BEYOND THE LINES

Creating a Leadership
Culture to Achieve
Extraordinary Results

To the Morimoto's,

Only High Standards Allowed!

Rusty Komori

BEYOND THE LINES

Creating a Leadership
Culture to Achieve
Extraordinary Results

◆

RUSTY KOMORI

LEGACY ISLE
PUBLISHING

ISBN 978-1-935690-97-9

Library of Congress Control Number: 2017957894

Front cover photo
Mikael Damkier/Dreamstime

Back cover photo
Darryl Watanabe

Design and production
Angela Wu-Ki

Legacy Isle Publishing
1000 Bishop St., Ste. 806
Honolulu, HI 96813
Toll-free 1-866-900-BOOK
info@legacyislepublishing.net
www.legacyislepublishing.net

Printed in the United States

CONTENTS

FOREWORD

Winners. Many people claim to be Winners, but very few actually are. As a performance physiologist and an expert in optimizing human performance, I study and train some of the most accomplished Winners in the world. In sports, winning a single championship at any level is very difficult, and often a lifetime endeavor. Winning a repeat, three-peat or four-peat is absolutely incredible and rarely happens.

Some of the greatest coaches in history have never won ten championships in a row. Bear Bryant, Dean Smith, Nick Saban, Phil Jackson, Coach K, and Joe Torre are all Hall of Famers, but not one of these great coaches has even come close to the consecutive number of championships that one unique coach has earned: By winning 22 consecutive state championships, Rusty Komori set a national record with the longest high school winning streak in U.S. history. As the renowned head coach of the Punahou School boys' varsity tennis team in Honolulu, Hawai'i, Coach Rusty will go down in history as the greatest high school coach, by record, in any sport.

Let's put this in perspective. Did you know there are approximately 18,435 high schools in the United States? If each high school has just eight varsity sports teams for boys and girls, there would be 294,960 high school teams playing in the U.S. each year. At Punahou School alone, there are currently 38 total varsity sports teams for boys and girls.

So why has no other coach accomplished this? What was Rusty's process in achieving it? Why him? What did he do as a leader? Many teams never win a state championship. The teams that do often win only periodically, for a variety of reasons. But how do you build a championship team and sustain a state championship streak for more than two decades? Well, Rusty did it and there's no reason why you can't do it too—if you have the correct process in place and understand what "real winning and real success" actually is. Looking back, his experience can be viewed as a 22-year coaching experiment in building and sustaining championship teams.

Beyond the Lines provides the details for any leader to help an organization achieve and sustain success. I have known Coach Rusty for nearly the entire duration of his unbelievable winning streak. I'm fortunate to know him as a friend, a mentor, and a highly accomplished coach who has achieved a level of success that supersedes sport. His principles and teachings have applications in sports, in business and in life.

Dr. Mark Kovacs
CEO, Kovacs Institute
Executive Director, International
Tennis Performance Association

CHAPTER 1

THE CHOICE IS YOURS

"Getting knocked down in life is a given. Getting up and moving forward is a choice." —Zig Ziglar

Success is not easy. If it were, everyone would be successful. It takes sacrifice, commitment, and relentless perseverance. Not everybody is willing to pay the price of success. It takes hard work but, more importantly, it takes smart work in order to achieve anything of significance. It goes without saying that life is very challenging. Let me make a prediction right now: You will have countless challenges in your own life. You've had many of them already, and there are definitely more on the way. The question is, do you deal with your challenges in a positive way? What's more, can you help others deal with their challenges in a positive way?

Before you can help others, you need to help yourself. This is not being selfish. When you're in an airplane and there's a change in cabin pressure, the flight attendants always advise passengers to put on their own oxygen masks before helping others with theirs. The principle is simple. You need to help yourself before you can effectively help others.

Do you know why there are so many bad leaders in the world? It's because nobody taught them how to be good ones. You can go to school to learn to be a good engineer or a good doctor. You can take golf lessons to become a good golfer. You can go to soccer practice and become a good soccer player. But most schools sadly don't offer classes in leadership, which would be extremely useful considering the number of people in leadership positions. Just think about how many team members are adversely affected by people who don't really know how to lead. Fortunately, you can make the choice right now to learn how to be a good, effective leader—and possibly a great one.

Knowledge is Power

There are many different types of people in the world. There are positive people and there are negative people. There are people who are confident and people with low self-esteem. There are people who are ambitious and people who are complacent. There are people who are disciplined and people who are undisciplined. There are people who react before thinking and people who think before reacting. There are people who care about others and people who only care about themselves. There are people who care about winning with integrity and people who want to win at all costs. What kind of leader would you want to follow? What kind of leader do you want to be? What kind of leader produces the best, consistent results for a team in business or sports?

Everyone has the power to make choices. You will either make good choices or bad ones, but they are your choices to make. And all of these choices have certain effects you need to be aware of. These effects cause your team to have good experiences or bad experiences. These effects cause your team to have good productivity or bad productivity. These effects can be healthy or unhealthy. These effects can cause you to win or lose. These effects can deepen the team bond or cause the team to deteriorate. And all of these effects happen because of a single choice. Your choice. Knowledge is powerful, and the more you learn, the better choices you can make. And these better choices can help you become a better leader in helping your team achieve their goals.

We have all been on a team at some point in time. We have observed the team leader, whether an employer or an athletic coach, and we can usually recall whether that leader was good, mediocre, or just plain bad. What did he do that was good? What could she have done better? Did the leader generate enthusiasm for you and the rest of the team? It's always interesting to reflect back on these experiences as a team member and imagine how things might have been different if you yourself were the team leader. Likewise, it's important for a leader to always put him or herself into team members' shoes to understand what they're thinking and feeling. If you're a team leader now, how do you think your current team members would grade and evaluate you?

Have you had a friend who had a bad experience in the workplace because the boss or manager treated her unfairly? Do you have a son or daughter or know of a child who was playing a sport and stopped playing because the coach led their team with questionable decision making, or other actions that made for a bad experience? Or perhaps you yourself have experienced these unfortunate situations in the workplace or in athletics? Whatever the scenario, it probably involved an unsuitable leader and the effects that he or she had on others. Making decisions and choices is a part of life and something we do every day. We have all made decisions in our life, both good and bad, and we learn from them. Great leaders are constantly learning, which helps make them even greater.

Mistakes vs. Failures

I know that mistakes will actually make you a stronger, better person. Everyone makes mistakes. It's part of living and learning. You learn what not to do the next time to avoid making the same mistake twice. There are causes and effects for every action. A leader may make a mistake that results in bad or unfortunate experiences for the team. And often times, these effects might cause team members to feel turned off. Too many times employees or athletes find themselves trapped in an unfortunate situation for too long, which may even lead them to look for a different profession or sport, all because of one person who affected them in a negative way. It would be sad if you were the person that caused others to feel this way. But what if you're a leader who just needs help and wants to improve—to become a stronger, more positive figure, rather than unintentionally or unknowingly leading in a counterproductive way? Then keep reading: This book will identify and explain eight keys to achieving success for people who lead teams in the workplace, in athletics, or anywhere else.

There's a big difference between mistakes and failures, but having the right perspective and mindset in dealing with either one is what really matters. A good leader knows that when you make a mistake, it's actually a learning experience. When you fail at something, it's an opportunity for improvement and future success. Henry Ford said, "Failure is an opportunity to more intelligently begin again." Failing at something and having it become a regret actually causes you to retreat and prevents you from moving forward. A leader will train his or her team members to view mistakes as learning experiences to improve themselves, instead of failing and feeling regret. Failure needs to be viewed as feedback. It's telling you what's not working so that you can figure out what does. If you don't try anything, you're absolutely guaranteed not to fail. You're also guaranteed not to grow. *Rich Dad, Poor Dad* author Robert Kiyosaki said, "Winners are not afraid of losing. But losers are. Failure is part of the process. People who avoid failure also avoid success."

It's imperative to learn from the experiences of others. In the long process of inventing the light bulb, Thomas Edison famously said, "I have not failed. I've just found 10,000 ways that won't work." Can you imagine if he didn't have the right perspective? We might all be living in darkness when the sun goes down. Michael Jordan, one of the greatest basketball players ever, said, "I've missed more than 9,000 shots in my career. I've lost almost 300 games. Twenty-six times, I was trusted to take the game-winning shot and missed. I've failed over and over and over again in my life. And that's why I succeed." Hockey great Wayne Gretzky said, "You'll always miss 100 percent of the shots you don't take."

It's important to try things to help yourself grow, and not have any regrets about trying them. Amazon founder and chairman Jeff Bezos said, "I wanted to project myself forward to age 80 and say, 'OK, I'm looking back on my life. I want to minimize the number of regrets I have.' And I knew that when I was 80, I was not going to regret having tried this. I was not going to regret trying to participate in this thing called the internet that I thought was going to be a really big deal. I knew that if I failed, I wouldn't regret that. But I knew the one thing I might regret is not ever having tried. I know that would haunt me every day."

In business, everything starts with the owner or CEO of a company. In sports, everything starts with the head coach. In both cases, this leader will be in a position to affect others on their team either in a positive or negative way, which directly affects the morale of the team and performance of every team member. There are so many diverse situations in which people lead other people. In education, for example, the president of a high school is the overall leader of that institution. The principals are in charge of the school supervisors. The supervisors are in charge of the school's teachers. The school's teachers are in charge of their students. For students to have the best possible experience and develop their full potential depends heavily on the leadership of the president and everyone in between. Think about your own experiences and how you would describe leaders that you've worked for in business or played for in sports. As a leader, you always have a choice in how you lead others.

Start vs. Finish

It's easy to make a choice to start something, but it's just as easy to stop doing it. Anyone can make a choice to go running or work out in the gym every day. Anyone can make a choice to eat healthier and go on a diet. Having the right intentions is good, but having the follow-through to do it every day is what counts. The concept is simple. Without commitment you will never start, but more important, without consistency you will never finish. We're all guilty of having started something without finishing it. If something is really important to you, you will find a way. If it's not important enough, you will find an excuse.

We are all presented with the same choice in decision making every single morning. That choice is whether or not to get out of bed when the alarm goes off. Some of us choose to get up and out of bed immediately, while some choose to hit snooze and stay in bed a while longer. The next choice we have is whether or not to make the bed. Some of us will, and some of us will choose to leave it unmade. Those of us who make that bed have just completed the first task of the day. This might not seem like much, but it really is. By completing the first task of the day, you're more likely to want to accomplish a second task, then a third, and so on. You will have a tendency to be more productive and put yourself in more favorable positions to accomplish things that day. And if you do have a bad day, you'll at least come home to a bed that's already made. So, wake up and make your bed! 🏀

CHAPTER 2

GREAT LEADERS ARE MADE

"A bird sitting on a tree is never afraid of the branch breaking, because her trust is not on the branch but on her own wings." —Anonymous

Great leaders are authentic and positive. They communicate well with people and inspire them to achieve both the task at hand and broader goals that they set. Great leaders have high standards, strong principles, and values. They help others strive for those same standards, principles, and values. Great leaders listen and create a safe, fun environment. They understand the importance of teamwork and giving their team members opportunities for growth. They celebrate the success of others. A great leader has a positive mindset. He or she creates a vision, then develops a detailed process to accomplish it. A great leader is always a mentor, who genuinely cares about the feelings and well-being of team members. A great leader is strong and tough in a crisis situation, and dependable, trusted, and respected by the entire team. People don't want to be "managed," after all—they want to be guided. They know that no matter how challenging a situation might be, they can trust the leader to make the best decisions for the team.

Anyone Can Be a Leader

In business, why is it that some assistant managers do not become good general managers? In football, why is it that some assistant coaches do not become good head coaches? There are numerous examples of successful offensive or defensive coordinators being promoted to head coach, expecting that their success as an assistant will carry over to their new role. But while there are some success stories, far too often people struggle in their new position and are terminated after just a year or two on the job.

The reason is clear. Anyone has the capacity to become a leader, but it doesn't mean that everyone wants to be or should be one. It's the same with parenting. Anyone can be a parent. But it doesn't mean that everyone wants to be or should be one. Some assistant managers are just good assistant managers—but will never be good general managers or CEOs. It's the same with an assistant football coach. An assistant coach might be an excellent offensive coordinator, but it doesn't guarantee that he'll be a good head coach. Promotions and advancement opportunities in business and sports are a good thing—but only if you're prepared to lead in that new role. Are you educating yourself correctly to be prepared for an opportunity when it presents itself? Are you learning as much as you can to expand your skill set and help develop your leadership potential?

Boss vs. Leader

There is a tremendous difference between a boss and a leader. A boss cares about work. A leader cares about people. A boss often instills fear, while a leader generates enthusiasm. A boss dictates, and a leader asks. A boss often says "I" and a leader often says "we." A boss often blames others when a breakdown occurs; a leader corrects the problem and takes responsibility for it. A boss micromanages; a leader delegates. A boss has his own way of doing things, while a leader is interested in finding new and better ways of doing things. A boss takes credit, while a leader gives credit. A boss knows how things are done; a leader coaches people by showing them how things are done. Employees often say they work *for* a boss instead of saying they work *with* the leader. Employees often think of themselves as coworkers in their boss's environment, instead of having the feeling they're part of a team with a strong leader. Which one are you? Which one do you want to be? If you're reading this book, it is clear to me that you care about people. You care enough to want to improve yourself as a leader, in order to really help the people on your team.

Simply being in a leadership position doesn't make you a leader. A CEO of a company might be the top executive—but might not be a true leader. The general manager of a business might be in a leadership position—but might not be a strong leader. The head coach of a sports team might run the program—but might not be an effective leader. They all have the authority and the title, but their team members still don't have the desire to follow them. People must want to follow their leaders. People need to like and respect their leaders.

Great leaders are likable and have good relationships with people. Great leaders listen, are aware, and can take the collective pulse to consistently know what's happening with their teams. Great leaders make everyone around them better. They are creative and innovative and always find ways to keep things fresh. They are able to consistently inspire and motivate people on the team to give their best at all times. Team members want to follow leaders who know where they're going, and who understand what goals they're striving to accomplish together. A great leader is fair and accountable for every action he or she takes, admitting when they've made a mistake and taking full responsibility for that decision. As a result, team members respect that leader even more, as no one needs to shoulder the blame but the leader himself. Great leaders have empathy and make people on their team feel like they belong. They genuinely want to help, support, and care for each team member—which in turn engenders further trust and loyalty.

By definition a good leader has followers. However, a great leader builds other great leaders. So many owners and CEOs of successful companies have mentored others to follow their lead on the path to success. Think about the many great coaches whose assistant coaches or former players became head coaches or successful leaders of other sports teams or businesses. A great leader, ultimately, builds more great leaders.

Only High Standards Allowed

Some leaders and coaches have their teams do things "above the line" instead of "below the line." My own version of that is to focus on simply having high standards rather than low ones. But however you say it, it really comes down to what standards you and your team choose to live by. A leader constantly strives for excellence and asks his or her team members to do the same. It's a matter of bettering yourself every day and having your team do the same—every single day. Focusing on performance goals definitely influences results. Everybody wants to win, get good results, and achieve certain goals. A great leader is never complacent. Instead, he or she seeks to outdo what was accomplished last year, or a month ago, or even yesterday. Great leaders are always looking for ways to improve both themselves and their teams. This is a habit that can almost become second nature, if you have high standards. But how do you actually accomplish this? The fact is, it is something that can be learned by following eight important keys.

Leadership is a skill that needs to be practiced. The eight keys that follow are critical for a team to achieve its goals, enjoy consistent results, and be in the best position to succeed. You cannot ask your team to do something that you aren't willing to do yourself. You must talk the talk and walk the walk. This is what great leaders do. It's how you will earn the respect of your team. You have heard it before, and it's true: You need to lead by example. And you don't have to be a coach to follow these keys; the parallels between coaching sports teams and business teams are countless.

Sir Richard Branson, founder of the Virgin Group, which controls more than 400 companies, is a firm believer in the correlation between sports and business. Branson said: "A lot of things learned through sport are transferable into other aspects of life. Skills acquired through tennis have been beneficial to business careers. Studies have shown that playing sports early in life is correlated with greater success in business, since competitive sports can teach discipline, teamwork, and leadership skills. One key lesson I've learned, which applies far beyond the tennis court, is to treat each point separately. It's critical to move on from the last mistake you made and focus on the next point, or in business, the next challenge. Tennis, like business, moves so quickly that if you dwell on the past for even a few minutes, an opportunity will have passed and the moment will be lost. You have to get into the right frame of mind in order to perform your best, and need to be able to put setbacks behind you instantly."

CHAPTER 3

THE FOUR PS OF SUCCESS

"A goal without a plan is just a wish."
—Antoine De Saint-Exupery

I was 24 when I was asked by our athletic director and tennis director to be the head coach for our Punahou School boys' varsity tennis team. I felt honored, but also felt a huge responsibility in helping develop these impressionable high school players. I wanted to be the best coach for them, build the best team, and give them the best team experience. I wanted to greatly enhance all of their lives in a positive way, by helping them become champions on the tennis court and champions in life. I wanted to help them see the bigger picture in life and not worry about the petty things that often cause distractions and unnecessary stress. Basically, I wanted us to be the best in everything we did. Obviously, I set high expectations for myself and needed to create a system to achieve this. This is when I developed a framework I refer to as the Four Ps—people + purpose + process = performance.

People

When you're a leader, you deal with people. Great leaders are not dictators. Great leaders enjoy working with people and creating a special team bond with them where everyone is important and everyone contributes equally. Great leaders genuinely care about them and will help them improve themselves in every possible way. Forming these bonds and connecting with people is imperative in order to build trust and loyalty. When you treat your people like family, the team begins to evolve into more than just a team—more like a second family. This is when the team members know their leader will do anything for them and they in turn will want to do anything for the leader.

Empathy is defined as the ability to understand and share the feelings of others. All great leaders have empathy for their team members but, more important, every team member knows that their leader possesses this empathy. This connection between the team members and their leader should be a powerful one. It's also a necessary one—it's how they know their leader is concerned with their well-being.

Purpose

People want to work toward something. More important, they want to work toward something significant. They are willing to work through and overcome any obstacle along the way to achieve it. Having a purpose in life gives them direction. It puts them on a certain street and hopefully they'll find the right way. And they often must do this together, as a team. But they need to know why it's important to have this mission and accomplish this goal. Why is this goal meaningful to achieve? It's your job as the leader to identify a clear purpose with your team and show them the right way. Give them a vision for the mission. They need to have a vivid picture in their minds so they can see the end result. This is the commitment you want your team to buy in to, so that they'll make the necessary sacrifices and commitment to begin the unwavering pursuit of this goal.

Process

Once you and your team have a purpose, and they understand why it's important to work towards the goal together, you need a detailed process to achieve that goal. In order for the process to work, you need discipline to execute it every single day. A day you waste is one you can never get back. You need to better yourself every day, and you need to get a little closer to achieving your goal every day. You need to make yourself take the right steps every single day, whether you "feel" like it or not. A thousand times I've heard people say, "I don't feel like doing it today" or "I'm not in the mood today." My response is always, "You don't feel like it? Well, you'd better get in the mood!" They need to understand that achieving this goal is something bigger than any one individual. This is something we must and need to do to help our team accomplish our goal. It's not acceptable for someone to be on a team and not do his or her part.

Every individual on a team needs to respect one another. And there will be respect if everyone is contributing and doing their part. The leader needs to make sure that this happens. You cannot have someone putting in the effort, doing their part, when someone else isn't. This is when people lose respect for each other. This is when they will also lose respect for the leader, if the leader doesn't address the problem and do something about it. Once there is respect, team members need to trust each other. They need to know that they have each other's back. They need to want to do something for you because you'd do the same thing for them. When every team member believes in the process and build the correct daily habits to commit to the process, the team is well on its way to achieving its goals.

Performance

As a leader, when you focus on your people, identify a clear purpose, and have a detailed process in place, you then give your team the best possible chance to perform to maximum potential every time. Consistent performance achieves success. Consistent performance allows you to sustain success. Whether it's an athlete competing on the basketball court or an employee selling cars at an auto dealership, consistency in performance is paramount. Average or even good teams fluctuate in their performance. They will win some and lose some. Great teams seem to win all the time. When they don't, it's viewed as a major upset, because great teams build high expectations from everyone, including themselves, to win. These great teams expect to win every game. It's a standard. It's because they have a system in place for success. Players and employees come and go, for whatever reason, but the next person up fills in, and the team keeps on winning without missing a beat.

When I developed the Four Ps, it made logical sense to me to have a system in place to do everything I set out to do, beginning on my first day at tennis practice as my team's head coach. Anything worthwhile that you want to achieve takes time. That's why every leader needs to have a plan for the team. That's why it's important to maximize every day. You get a little bit closer each day in accomplishing your goals. The Four Ps provide the framework and the Eight Keys provide the details. As we review these Eight Keys of achieving success, please reflect on how my examples in sports directly correlate to the many leadership situations that we encounter in life. 🎾

◆

CHAPTER 4

KEY NO. 1:
THE CHARACTER OF A CHAMPION

*"Sometimes the smallest step in the right direction
ends up being the biggest step of your life."*
—Naeem Callaway

In sports, every coach can help build and improve the character of the athletes, which can help them achieve success in both their sport and in life. In business, every leader can help build and improve the character of team members, which will help them in the workplace and in their lives. The coaching philosophy for all coaches in all sports should be striving to develop champion athletes of good character. The same leadership philosophy can be applied in the workplace to help employees be the best people they can be—representing the organization in the best possible way. Focusing on building character gives everyone the chance to perform to maximum ability and potential. They will be thinking and acting in ways to put themselves and the team in the best possible position for success. This needs to be done as early and consistently as possible.

In soccer, you often see a team of five- and six-year-olds being coached by a parent with limited knowledge of the sport. This parent coach has a critically important role to instill certain things in these young players. The players need to have fun, and they need to learn the basic fundamentals of soccer and the importance of teamwork. Most important, they need to start building the kind of character that will help them in athletics and in life. But much too often, the parent coach is focusing on winning and only on winning. This can have adverse effects as these young boys and girls begin to think that only winning is important. This might lead them to have a mindset to win at all costs. This might cause them to cheat to win. It might cause them to be mean to their opponents in order to win. It can even cause them to be mean to their own teammates, if they see that only the stronger players are consistently in the starting lineup. It might cause an unhealthy climate among teammates, instead of creating a healthy climate where individuals are working together and helping each other improve.

We sometimes wonder whether professional athletes are indeed good role models. We see some of these professionals reach the pinnacle of achievement and success in their sport, and then see them fall from grace, the direct result of flawed character. It's obvious that these professionals are exceptional athletes, yet individuals of questionable character. This might even keep them from playing or competing at an even higher level and achieving even greater success. Can you imagine these athletes going back in time to when they were five years old, playing their sport for the first time, and having a coach instill in them that character should be their number one focus, that they are to win with humility and lose with grace. How much different would each of their lives be today?

Develop Your Philosophy

All coaches or leaders should have a philosophy that they instill in their teams. But is their coaching philosophy effective in achieving the goals and results they want for their team? Or are they going about it the wrong way? Are they focused too much on winning, which might be hindering their team from achieving its maximum potential? Is their philosophy helping or hurting the development of the members and the team as a whole? A leader needs to first identify what is really important for his or her team. What can you do to put your team in the best position to succeed? What degree of excellence do you want for your team? And how do you then introduce the correct process for coaching and leading your team? What legacy do you want to leave to your team members? When I became head coach of the Punahou School boys' varsity tennis program back in 1994, my team philosophy was to develop champion athletes of great character first, and great tennis players second. I shared with my team that it is most important for us to exhibit character, respect for others and ourselves, unimpeachable ethics and integrity, and a constant striving for excellence. I already had some good athletes, but what's a good athlete with poor discipline or bad character? Definitely, not one that I'd be proud of. I wanted to set a high standard for that 1994 team, to serve as a model for teams to follow for years to come.

I don't agree when people say it doesn't matter if you win or lose—"just have fun and enjoy the experience." It does matter if you win or lose. Winning is important. If it weren't, we wouldn't keep score. But you need to do it correctly. In my youth, I remember having a Snoopy tennis poster in my room with the message, "It doesn't matter if you win or lose, until you lose." I learned something very important about myself by competing in baseball, soccer, and tennis. I learned that winning was fine with me, but I absolutely hated to lose. It's something that I still feel to this day. Trying your very best to win is a good thing in that it requires you to formulate a plan, execute a strategy, deal with stress and adversity, solve problems, and put yourself and your team in the best position to be successful.

I also don't agree with giving trophies to everyone who participates in a tournament. It devalues the meaning of a trophy for those who work hard to earn one. What's more, those who don't win—especially those who finish last—are embarrassed because they know they really don't deserve a trophy. At our annual Punahou School Junior Novice Tennis

Tournament, we displayed the trophies on the first day of the tournament where the players and their parents could see them when they checked in. They noticed that there were a few big, tall trophies and others that were much smaller. Upon closer inspection, they also noticed that the big, tall ones were the sportsmanship trophies and the smaller ones were for the champions and finalists. Our top priority was to show how important sportsmanship and good character is. Our participants began to understand this too—they all wanted to be chosen as the sportsmanship winner and take that big, beautiful trophy home. The effect was significant. Our top priority became their top priority, because they knew the tournament committee valued sportsmanship more than winning. Consequently, their good attitude and behavior and respect for opponents helped all of them perform at a much higher level—which then put them in more favorable positions to win.

Constant Thirst For Growth

Many people have asked me about the sports I've played, and how I developed my own character and leadership traits. In my youth, I first played baseball. I liked the sport because many of my school friends played and it was fun learning skills such as throwing, pitching, catching, and batting. Thanks to baseball, my hand-eye coordination improved a great deal, and I especially liked pitching and playing second base. After a few years of baseball, soccer became an interest of mine because, again, many of my friends played that sport. I liked the movement and fast action, although I didn't care too much for all the running involved. Yes, I know—if you play soccer, you run all the time. My footwork, movement, and conditioning were greatly improved from playing soccer, as well they should have with all that running in practice and in games. After a few years of soccer, I began to take an interest in tennis. My mom started playing and I would go to the tennis courts with her to try it myself. It looks easy enough on television, so I thought it would be no problem for me. I quickly realized how difficult and challenging a sport tennis is. I began to visualize how much fun it is to hit home runs in baseball and started trying to do the same thing on the tennis court. Mom immediately put a stop to that and said that if I wanted to play tennis, I would have to learn the sport correctly by taking tennis lessons. So I did and quickly realized that the skills I'd learned in baseball and soccer greatly complemented what I was learning in tennis. I began to improve tremendously in the sport, when I realized that all I had to do to win was hit the ball in one more time than my opponent. I thought to myself, *I can do that!* So the hand-eye skills that I practiced in baseball and the footwork skills I learned in soccer helped me in tennis.

In baseball and soccer, I'd observed that you can have one or two great players on your team and still lose a lot of games. But in tennis, it all depends on me—I can't blame anyone else if I lose. I earn all the glory when I win, and I accept all the blame when I lose. It was also clear that if I wanted to be great at tennis, I could be. No one else could tell me that I couldn't be great because it all depended on me. I liked having this control over my own destiny even though I started playing tennis relatively late, in the ninth grade. In high school, varsity soccer and varsity tennis had overlapping seasons, which forced me to choose one sport over the other. I chose to play varsity soccer for Damien Memorial High School in the ninth grade, while I continued to practice tennis as much as I could. I began to enter tennis competitions and won my first two novice tournaments in the same week. Because I won at the novice level, I soon had to move up into open tournaments and compete against the top-ranked players in the state of Hawai'i, many of whom had been playing tennis since the age of five or six.

Obviously, I had a lot of catching up to do, but I really enjoyed the challenge of competing one on one in singles. I then began to play varsity tennis for my high school, from tenth grade all the way until I graduated. My goal during my first year of competitive play in tournaments was to be one of the top 20 in Hawai'i. At the end of the year, I was ranked number 18. My goal during junior year was to make the top ten. I was ranked number eight. My goal during my senior year was to make the top five. I achieved a number four state ranking and earned a partial tennis scholarship to attend Creighton University in Omaha, Nebraska. That was the first year that Creighton coach Ed Hubbs said the school could offer partial tennis scholarships. So I chose Creighton for its good academic reputation and the opportunity to compete in Division I college tennis. As an entering freshman, I flew by myself to Omaha where—not having visited beforehand—I expected to find red barns and farmers wearing overalls. But as the plane came in for a landing, I looked out the window and saw a big attractive city down below, and I just knew that my college experience was going to be a good one.

My personal character development began with strict discipline from my parents, mainly my mom, and was also influenced by the very strict Christian school that I attended from preschool until eighth grade. After that came Damien High, which was considered the strictest Catholic school in the state. Needless to say, a sense of discipline and respect for others were instilled in me from the start. Through those elementary, intermediate, and high school years, I had observed my baseball, soccer, and tennis coaches closely. I learned many positives and negatives about what to do and what not to do as a coach. I learned about the variety of ways they made sports fun—including hard work. I learned how important communication is between coach and players, and how to bring out the best in team members. I learned that not everyone can be coached the same way, because players have different personalities, and different triggers must be used to get players to respond optimally and to the best of their ability. Of all the coaches I had during this time, I felt the biggest impact and learned the most from Coach Ed at Creighton. Coming from Hawai'i and going to Nebraska was a big change for me, but also an exciting one. I was independent and had to learn to do things, including my own laundry, for the first time.

When I first started with Creighton's tennis program, Coach Ed had entered our team in the Nebraska Open tournament in Omaha, where many other college teams would compete. This was Coach Ed's first real look at his new players, other than seeing them on a Betamax recruiting tape. Yes, Betamax—the technology before the VHS tape. (And yes, VHS was the technology before DVDs, which came before Blu-ray.) Because of the many freshman orientation events I had to attend, I didn't have much time to practice tennis before the tournament. After winning my first two rounds, I developed a big blister on my right hand during my third round match. I'm right-handed and had played with blisters before, as many other players have, but this one was really bad. The blister was in the middle of my hand, and it was ripping and bleeding along the crease of my palm with every shot I made. Needless to say, it was very painful. But even more painful was the fact that I was losing to an extremely tough opponent, and the blister was my excuse. I retired the match in the second set and went back to my Swanson Hall dorm room. At 5:30 the next morning, my phone rang. It was Coach Ed, telling me to get my butt into his office in ten minutes. I brushed my teeth and ran fearfully over to his office, suspecting that my retiring a third round match because of a blister might be unacceptable in college.

"Did you retire a match because of a blister?" Coach Ed demanded as soon as I walked in. "Where is this blister?" I held out my hand and he pulled it towards him, tapping his index finger on the blister. "Does this hurt?" he asked. I didn't want to admit it at first, but then nodded. He simply said, "Never, ever retire a match because of a blister." I assured him that it would never happen again and left his office to head to the tennis courts for our early morning practice. And, yes, I did tape up my hand and prepare myself for a tough session.

The following year we played a match outdoors in Missouri after spring break, when the temperature dropped 25 degrees in two hours. It began to snow in flurries, and it was freezing. It was easily the coldest match I have ever played. I wore two T-shirts, a long-sleeved shirt, a reverse weave sweatshirt, and my team jacket over all of that. I also wore double socks, my shorts, cotton sweatpants, and my team sweatpants over it all, and it was still freezing cold. My ears were numb and I was feeling miserable, and I definitely didn't want to be out there playing tennis. My opponent beat me 6–2, 6–2, because I put up no fight against someone I should have beaten by that score.

Five minutes or so after every match I played, Coach Ed would usually stop to talk with me. This time, as I sat outside the court, watching my teammates play, trying to get warm, he walked by without saying a word. I immediately knew I had done something unacceptable again, and I feared what he might do this time. He walked by again without saying a word, but then doubled back and began yelling at me in front of everyone. He said I was weak and gutless and some other words I'm sure he invented, a tirade that seemed to last nearly five minutes. Then he walked away, without my getting in a single word. As I sat there digesting what had just happened, I realized everything he'd said was true. I *was* weak and gutless and all the other words he'd invented. It was an extremely important turning point for me, and I began to understand Coach Ed completely. He was trying to make me tougher and stronger, a player who could be the leader of our team. I subsequently became team captain for the next two years. I figured out that Coach Ed was really helping mold my character. He didn't want me making excuses because of a blister or cold weather. He wanted me to give it my best no matter how tough, distressing, or uncomfortable the situation might be. He knew that my teammates would emulate me and begin to have that same fight.

Character is Contagious

Great leaders are not born. They are made. They are made through the influence of others. This is what shapes their character. It's the effect that others had on them and it becomes contagious. Let's look at Bill Belichick, head coach of the

National Football League's New England Patriots since 2000. Seven of his assistant coaches became NFL head coaches. Seven of his assistant coaches became NCAA Division I head coaches. And 19 assistant coaches or executives under him have become assistant head coaches, coordinators, or executives in the NFL. For all these people, it was the experiences they encountered on their own journeys through life that shaped them into who they are today. They learn what works and what doesn't. They learn what is effective and what is ineffective. This is how great leaders are made. This is how you can help build other great leaders by affecting your team members in a positive way.

Obviously, good parenting is very important in establishing a strong foundation for building character in a child. It doesn't matter if a coach begins his coaching relationship with a kid at age five, ten, or 15, parents definitely play a key role from the beginning. And they continue to play that role in helping reinforce the right character traits the child learns through sports. A good coach with the right values can greatly enhance and build on that early foundation. Did you know that a child playing sports spends more time with the coach and team than he or she spends in school with a math, science, or English teacher? This means that the coach has a major impact on the child. It is both a huge responsibility and a great opportunity to help instill the correct discipline, values, and morals that shape the players' character. Likewise, the general manager of a business also needs to instill the correct discipline, values, and morals in the staff, which will strengthen the team bond and help the team accomplish its goals. Putting your team members in the best position to be successful, doing it the right way with great character, becomes contagious and fosters a positive, safe, and fun environment.

Champions Are Defined by Others

Great leaders breed more leaders. That's what Coach Ed did for me at Creighton. On April 9, 2014, I flew back to Omaha from Hawai'i as the very first tennis player inducted into Creighton University's Hall of Fame. During my Hall of Fame speech in front of nearly 1,000 people, I was so very proud to highlight Coach Ed (I had him stand to be recognized by everyone there) as the main reason for me winning 130 matches in the number one and number two positions in my college career. Everything I learned from him were priceless gifts for me to use as guidelines in coaching my own teams. Respecting others, having integrity, and being courageous, ethical, resilient, determined, inspirational, honest, and positive were a few of the many character traits that Coach Ed instilled in me. His focus and dedication in helping me compete, act, think, and behave properly unlocked my potential in tennis and shaped my leadership qualities.

After graduating from Creighton with a communications degree in 1991, I came back to Hawai'i, became certified with the United States Professional Tennis Association, and began teaching tennis. My intent was to pursue law and become an attorney, but the lawyers who took lessons from me wore glasses that appeared three inches thick. I asked them what their typical day was like and they all said that they read all day in the office. But I didn't want to read things I had to read; I wanted to read things I liked to read. So that was the end of my pursuit of law, and I continued teaching tennis instead. I quickly began to develop many of our state's top-ranked junior players. Plus, I got to wear shorts and be outdoors in Hawai'i every day.

In 1994, I was offered the head coaching position for the Punahou boys' varsity tennis team. I was 24 years old. The most important thing I wanted to do was instill the importance of character in my team. I told them we would strive constantly for excellence by having integrity, ethics, honor, humility, positivity, respect for others, courage, inspiration, and the determination to compete with every ounce of our being. I told the boys I only had two team rules—Lateness and Listening. And while they were all listening, I quickly added that we would have no verbal, ball, or racket abuse. In order to play our best tennis, we needed to control our tongues, hands, and thoughts at all times. If we can do this, we have a great chance of controlling the tennis ball. Any violation of the Listening rule would result in 100 push-ups. Any violation of the Lateness rule would result in running "snakes" on the bleachers. It's simply amazing how quickly doing 100 push-ups or running snakes cures the listening and lateness problems.

Self-discipline and team discipline became important goals for me to constantly instill and enhance in my players. Doing the right thing whether or not someone is watching should make no difference. I gave my team an example by telling them if they walked by a piece of trash without picking it up, someone would see that and assume that our entire team did it. Instead, it's very easy to pick up that piece of trash, drop it in a garbage can, and continue on your way. Another example happens when it rains and we need to dry the tennis court. I told my players that we should be proactive by grabbing a squeegee and being the first ones on the court to help dry it off, rather than waiting for our opponents or someone else to do it. It's the simple, little things that makes big differences. It's a discipline that must be carried out on and off the tennis court.

Two weeks into our season, we were up against a much weaker school, and I noticed one of my senior singles players competing in a match on center court and badly disrespecting his opponent. I closely observed his behavior during the match, in which he acted as if his opponent was absolutely wasting his time. My player served and his opponent missed the return. The opponent served and my player made the return. His opponent hit the next shot out. This was a pattern that happened over and over again throughout the match. After finishing the match in a very brief 25 minutes, my player walked up to me bragging, "Coach, I won, 6–0, 6–0!" My response was: "All right, you're off the team." When he asked why, a shocked and confused look on his face, I said I didn't want any of my players behaving and acting that way— that his actions were shameful and disrespectful and would poison our team. I sent him home, and he telephoned me later that night to apologize and asked if he could rejoin the team. I told him I'd talk with the team in practice, and that *they* would decide whether to give him a second chance. The next day, I shared our conversation with the team and let them talk among themselves for five minutes. I asked the boys what they'd decided and they said they wanted to give him a second chance. I said I'd call him that evening with the news, and he could rejoin the team the next day. When he came back—wow, what a turnaround in attitude! He apologized to the entire team for his actions during his match, and after that the difference was like night and day. He got it and understood clearly what Punahou boys' varsity tennis was all about.

This incident unsettled some of the younger players on the team, who looked up to this senior player and figured if it could happen to him, it could happen to anyone. So it was a valuable learning experience for both the individual and the team. They began to learn that our team was not so much about our victories as it was about our character. Of course, we're going to strive to win, but by doing it the right way. Most athletes want to be good at their sport, and some athletes want to achieve mastery. But it isn't done with an attitude and focus on winning at all costs. It's done with an attitude and focus on simply being a good person, and striving for excellence with character—which incidentally unlocks their true potential as athletes.

The Chris Ma Story

In 1994, my first year as Punahou's head tennis coach, I had a freshman player named Chris Ma, who beat all of our top senior players in tryouts to earn the number one spot on our team. Chris had been ranked number one in the state of Hawai'i ever since he began competing in the ten and under division. He already had many good character traits instilled in him by his parents and previous coach and was well-liked by everyone. I felt it was my responsibility to continue to enhance and reinforce the discipline and character traits that were important to me in building the identity of our team. This philosophy would help not only Chris but also every member on our team.

Once our tryouts were completed, I needed to submit a team roster at our coaches meeting, deciding which players would represent our team in singles and doubles. From 12 players, I needed to select four singles players and four doubles teams. I had five players picked for singles but still needed to decide who would play doubles. As I sat on the bleachers mulling it over, Chris walked by and asked me what I was thinking about. I shared with him the dilemma I faced in deciding who played singles and doubles. I was trying to put myself in their shoes, and to make certain that everything was done fairly to give both the players and the team the best possible experience. I explained to Chris that we had two seniors who had won the state doubles championship the previous year, and I imagined they now wanted a chance to win a singles championship. We had another senior who was ranked number one in the state in the boys 18s division; if I were him, I would also want the opportunity to play for a singles championship. And we had another senior who was really exceptional at singles but often struggled in doubles.

And then there was Chris, who had beaten all four seniors to earn the number-one spot on our team. In effect, this gave me five players that I really wanted to play singles, but one of whom would need to play doubles. Chris completely understood my dilemma and without hesitation said, "Coach, I'll play doubles!" I reminded him he had earned the right to be our number one singles player, and I assumed he would want to—in fact, would expect to—play singles.

"If I can help the team in doubles," he replied, "then I'll play doubles and the four seniors can have their chance in singles." I was caught completely off guard—this would solve my dilemma and let me submit our team lineup for the season.

Chris's offer showed me how much of a team player

he was, and how selfless he was in helping our team in any way possible. At our team meeting the next day, I shared the dilemma I faced and gave high praise to Chris in front of everyone—it was the perfect opportunity to demonstrate that we should always do what was best for the team, rather than for ourselves. As great as Chris was in tennis, he showed he was even better as a person. Due to his character, he quickly earned respect from me and everyone else he came into contact with. He went on to become the model player for our tennis program, and I would share the Chris Ma story with every team that followed.

And by the way, Chris partnered with a senior that year—a player who had lost to his teammates in the previous state doubles championship—and went undefeated the entire season, winning the state doubles championship final, 6–0, 6–1. 🎾

CHAPTER 5

Key No. 2:
Discipline Drives Performance

"When you want something you've never had,
you have to do something you've never done."
—Thomas Jefferson

Discipline can be defined as the practice of training people to obey rules or a code of behavior. Let me be clear—discipline is training others to act, think, and behave correctly. It is not punishment. Goals cannot be achieved without discipline. We all feel differently every day. You can't allow yourself to only do certain things when you feel good. You need to have the discipline to do things when you don't feel like it. In other words, having discipline means forcing yourself to behave differently than you feel. If you only did things when you felt good, you wouldn't get much done. I believe that 90 percent of discipline is just showing up. Disciplined people keep their promises and commitments. They do not procrastinate. They know that discipline means *doing* things. It's getting things done. It must become a habit, one that is done consistently to achieve one's goals.

Simple Rules, Clear Consequences

A great leader establishes simple rules with clear consequences. My two rules are Lateness and Listening. These are two very simple rules but extremely meaningful in sports, business, and life. It is critically important to explain the consequences clearly to your team, so that there's no confusion if any violations of team rules occur. One minute late is late. For our team, the consequences of being late was five snake runs on the stadium bleachers. Snakes is a conditioning exercise in which you run up the stairs, across the bleachers, down the next set of stairs, across the next section of bleachers, up the next set of stairs, and so on. If a player is caught not listening, the first offense earns 50 push-ups. If it happens a second time or any time thereafter, it's 100 push-ups. It's amazing how 100 push-ups quickly solves a listening problem, or how five snake runs on the bleachers cures the lateness problem. I chose these consequences to help build both their strength and conditioning, which the players need to be doing anyway. The method of discipline needs to be a positive one that will help them improve, rather than a consequence that is only viewed negatively.

During our practices, we often played various tennis games for conditioning and also employed a variety of footwork exercises. Communication is critical so that conditioning is not mistaken as punishment. For example, I would say, "When we finish this next game, everyone does ten sprints, but the winning team can choose to do only half that number." When explained correctly in this way, winning the game and doing half the conditioning is viewed as a reward. Compare that with saying, "The winners of this next game can do five sprints, while the losers will do ten." In this sense, losing and conditioning are paired negatively and seen as punishment. I don't even use the term "losers." Rather, I use the word "unfortunates." As mentioned earlier, some of our disciplines involve no racket, ball, or verbal abuse. I would always say, "We can do 99 things right, but if we do one thing wrong, then everyone will only remember that one thing." This is important because this philosophy holds the entire team accountable. If there's a lapse in judgement by a player who swears out loud or commits verbal abuse that others can hear, it appears to outsiders that all of our players swears like that. This discipline is important because it doesn't matter if it's my number one player or my number 12 player committing the verbal abuse. Everyone lives by the same standard.

Accountability is Everything

The rules are for everyone on your team, and everyone must hold each other accountable. It is discipline that must be enforced consistently. Otherwise your rules become meaningless and your respect will begin to deteriorate. Everyone is treated the same and you, as the leader, must not play favorites. This allows the whole team to have the best possible experience, and not just the top athletes while the rest of the team experiences an erosion in morale—one in which the team starts feeling like less of a team. Rules and discipline are imperative in building the framework for character traits you want to instill and enhance in your team. You can't afford to send mixed messages by enforcing the rules only part of the time. But everything you do must still be reasonable and fair. Put yourself in their shoes so that you can never be accused of being otherwise.

For example, practice for our tennis team started at 3:45 p.m. Remember, one minute late is late. At 3:44, all of my players present were aware of the time and calculating who wasn't there, and how many snakes that individual would be doing on the bleachers. Often times we'd see players cutting it close, sprinting to be with the team before the clock struck 3:46, and thereby sparing themselves the additional exercise. The point, of course, is punctuality. They were learning that it's important to be punctual. Punctuality is necessary and something that would definitely help them in life beyond tennis.

How many times does a coach try to explain a drill to the team while some of the players talk with each other and ignore what the coach is saying? This is when the listening rule comes in handy. If I'm explaining the next exercise and I say, "Austin and Jake will be playing the crosscourt forehand game on court four," and Austin says, "Which court?" then my response is: "You weren't listening. That's a violation of our listening rule. That's 100 push-ups." This is what I mean when I say that 100 push-ups cures the listening problem. Just think how much better your team will be focused and listening to what you say the next time you explain a drill or game. This is a discipline and standard that must be consistently enforced by the leader.

Lead with Positivity

I'm a big believer in noticing a team member doing something good and highlighting that action or behavior to every other member of the team. People do good deeds all the time. Compliment them. Acknowledge them. This becomes contagious because it reinforces to others what you are striving for. Other team members will have a greater tendency to want to do good deeds as well. I'm all about attention to detail, so when it's time to collect all the tennis balls after practice, and I see Freddie going out of his way to run two courts over to get one lonely ball, I make it known to everyone that this kind of detail is what I appreciate. It is a standard of excellence. When it's ball collection time at the next practice, more players will have a tendency to follow Freddie's lead.

I love highlighting a player who encourages a teammate who might be struggling mentally or emotionally that day. It's all about helping and supporting each other by doing things that you would want others to do for you. Many leaders catch a team member doing something wrong, and then embarrass that person by admonishing him or her loudly and generally making a scene. This isn't good. I do the opposite. When I catch a team member doing something wrong, I talk with him discreetly at a low volume. But when I see a team member emulating something we're striving for, I make certain that everybody hears me. This is healthy for everyone and helps the team focus on what to do, as opposed to what not to do.

The Jason Chang Story

Here's an exception in talking discreetly to a player at a low volume. During my first year as head coach of Punahou's boys varsity, I received a phone call a week after the state championships.

"Hi, Coach Rusty! It's Jason Chang. I was wondering if you had any time in your schedule to work me in for private lessons?"

"Jason," I replied, "you know about my standards and expectations in behavior from students. I've watched you compete in the tournaments and I know you're a good player, but I'm not sure it would work out. To be honest, your behavior and attitude are the opposite of what I try to teach."

"I'm really willing to try," he answered. When I heard that, I decided to give him an opportunity and worked him into my schedule for lessons. I knew it was going to be a big challenge to help him make the kind of turnaround that would help his tennis and ultimately impact his life. I also knew it would be a process that would take some time.

Jason was just finishing tenth grade when I started teaching him privately. He was already a good player, ranked number eight in Hawai'i in the boys 16s division and number one on 'Iolani School's boys' varsity tennis team. Prior to that phone call, what I'd observed from Jason in tournaments was extremely poor behavior and bad discipline. He frequently committed all three abuses—verbal, racket, and ball—and often yelled and caused a scene on the tennis court during competition. It was bad. And this is why I responded the way I did when he called. He was definitely on the wrong end of the spectrum and needed major help and guidance. Jason played with a lot of passion and fire, because he loved tennis. But nobody had taught him discipline—how to control himself mentally and emotionally. During our first lesson, I remember clearly explaining to him the Listening and Lateness rules; that there would be no verbal, ball, or racket abuse; and what the consequences would be if there ever were. Jason was willing to make a change, and I told him that it would take some time for him to completely control his behavior.

So the process began. There were definitely some flare-ups along the way and phone calls to his parents, especially after I added Jason to my advanced group training lesson with his peers. They were all extremely competitive with each other, because they all hated to lose, even in our group tennis lessons. They all played against each other in tournaments and were all highly ranked in Hawai'i. I knew this was exactly what Jason needed every single week, and he consistently showed up for his weekly private lessons and weekly group lessons. Having a high standard for Jason to strive for, plus the opportunity to interact with peers who were all striving for our standard of excellence, really helped reshape his focus and priorities. I told him he was nowhere near reaching his potential in tennis, because he held himself back by letting unnecessary situations affect his performance. When he would fall behind in a match, for instance, he played differently than he did when he was winning. My challenge to him was to compete the same way whether he was losing, winning, or tied, and to keep a good attitude and control his behavior at all times. Hearing these things over and over again every week had a huge positive effect on Jason. I told him he needed to adjust his focus from competing against opponents to bettering himself. He needed to realize that he was not going to win every single point and every match for the rest of his life. But he could give it his best by trying to put himself in a position to win. That, after all, is what makes sports exciting—being in a position to win. Sometimes we win and sometimes we don't, and that's OK.

In 1996, his senior year, Jason competed in singles at the state championship tournament in Wailea, Maui. In the semifinals, he played another one of my players, Chris Ma, who was then in his junior year. The match lasted just under three hours. It was an incredible display of groundstrokes, movement, and heart. Chris defeated Jason, 7–5, 7–5. They both showed much respect for one other, and it was a great test to see how far Jason had come—and for him to see what the bright end of the spectrum looks like. Needless to say, I was extremely proud of him and his display of character in the face of such stress and adversity. Jason's transformation was validated when he earned the number one ranking in the statewide boys 18s division after he graduated from 'Iolani.

My training and guidance for him didn't end there; we now started to prepare him for college tennis at the University of California at Irvine. That summer, during a group training lesson, Jason was having a bad day, had a major flare-up, and threw his racket against the fence on the far side of the tennis court.

"Jason, get out of here!" I yelled across the court. "You're number one, but you still can't control yourself after all this time and effort. Get out! In fact, leave your rackets here and just start running around the block!"

Now the street where our tennis courts are located was circular, and running one time around the circle covered 1.1 miles. I continued the group training, and all the other players were working extra hard, probably because they'd never heard me yell like that before. But they all knew why I did it, and how Jason had been before I started his lessons. And they knew that if a rule was violated, it didn't matter if you were ranked number one or number 30. It was a great reminder for all of them of the high standards we set for ourselves. The younger players were also reminded of the consequences when rules were violated. As I continued the lesson, I saw Jason running by, trying to make sure that I saw him. I did but looked away and he continued running—a second time then a third time around. After he'd covered 3.3 miles, I told Jason to get back on the court to resume training. He was back on track, probably frightened that I yelled at him in front of everyone, and never had a flare-up after that. Today, Jason is a doctor and the youngest chief medical director for the Rehabilitation Hospital of the Pacific in Honolulu, married with three children. I am so very proud of the person he became, and he has shared with me that he leads his medical staff with many of the same principles, rules, disciplines, and standards that he learned in tennis. 🎾

CHAPTER 6

KEY NO. 3: ALWAYS IN CONTROL

"People who say it cannot be done should not interrupt those who are doing it."
—George Bernard Shaw

It's inevitable—there are some things over which you have no control. You're in a traffic accident because the guy behind you is careless and runs into you. You're stuck in bumper-to-bumper traffic because someone else had an accident. Your flight is delayed or even canceled because of bad weather. But while situations like this are completely out of your control, what you can control is your own reaction. You can choose to react rationally or irrationally. You can choose to react by stressing about the situation, or by staying calm and letting go of stress.

So how does an effective leader respond at such times? She controls the situation rather than letting the situation control her. One of the best ways to do this is to expect the unexpected. It's imperative to envision the different turns that a certain situation can take—and to plan for how you will deal with them. Unforeseen circumstances can happen, and you need to be prepared for all scenarios. What if a team member gets injured? Or if someone gets sick? What if you fall behind early in a game? What if you establish a big lead? What if the officials make bad calls against your team? What if the entire crowd is against you? What about the weather? You

37

need to accept it and deal with it, rather than complain and make excuses. Both teams must deal with challenging weather conditions; the key is to get through them better than your opponent. The point is, great leaders are well-prepared for any of multiple scenarios that can and will happen. They already have a plan B and plan C and have trained their team members to prepare and respond in the same way.

Learn to Differentiate

Let's consider our choices in different situations. We can plan ahead or we can choose to be unprepared. We can accept a bad attitude or choose to assume a good one. We can choose to behave appropriately or choose to behave badly. We can choose to be lazy, or we can choose to give 100 percent effort. We can choose to give up or we can choose to bounce back. We can choose to respect others or we can choose to disrespect them. We can choose to be weak or we can choose to be strong and tough. We can make do with low standards, or choose a high standard of excellence for ourselves. We can choose to be distracted or we can choose to focus on what we want to accomplish. We can choose to rush things or we can choose to be patient. We can choose to cheat or we can choose to have integrity. We can choose to lie or we can choose to be honest. We can choose to be mean to others or we can choose to be kind. We can choose to be selfish or we can choose to be humble. We can choose to be bad sports or choose to exhibit sportsmanship.

In other words, there are many things that team members can control for themselves. And as their leader, you need to identify and explain that they do have choices—and consequences for their choices. Leaders need to be role models and choose the proper choices by walking the walk in order to talk the talk. It determines the identity you want for your team and the legacy you want to leave them with.

Read Emotions

Emotional awareness means being aware of other people's emotions as well as your own. A strong leader must always remember to base decisions on reason, not emotion. Using your emotional awareness is always better than reacting quickly and regretting it later. Never do something permanently foolish just because you're temporarily upset. This starts with the leader and trickles down to the members of the team. I have watched countless sports competitions where one team is losing—not because the other team is doing things to win, but because the losing team is defeating themselves with their negative attitude. So when you find yourself in a hole, stop digging. And if your team is on the winning end of this scenario, don't get in the way of your opponent when they're shooting themselves in the collective foot!

Having emotional awareness requires having control of your thoughts. When you have control over your own thinking, you can have control over your life. Leaders with emotional awareness are conscious of their own emotions and able to manage their feelings properly. Maintaining poise, no matter what the situation may be, is paramount. Leaders also need to be aware of the emotional state of other people. Understanding why a person is behaving or feeling a certain way is important in being able to help them. Having empathy for that person will create a connection with them, when they realize that you understand why they're feeling the way they are.

Ignore the Noise

Let's face it: Apart from the winning team and its supporters, many people enjoy seeing a victorious streak come to an end. They want to see a champion defeated by an underdog. They want to see a number one team lose. They're jealous of your success. And when your team is in the public eye, the sports media can add pressure by highlighting your accomplishments. All of this might add unnecessary stress to your team. It's up to you to keep the focus on what's important to the team's success. Adverse situations should narrow the focus of the team members on what they want to accomplish together. There will always be distractions and noise, both externally and internally, but you need to keep the focus on what you can control. I always have 12 boys on my varsity team, but I never have the same 12 boys the following year because the seniors graduate. So winning the state championship, then having some of those players return while adding new players who make the team, creates a whole new team of 12. The fact is, not all 12 of them won that state championship. I explain to them that this is why we're not really defending a championship—we're trying to win a championship with a new team of players. This becomes their focus, because they understand that they want to earn a championship together as a new team. This minimizes the pressure of defending a championship; it keeps a proper perspective on what they want to achieve together as a team goal.

You Own Your Thoughts

Control your thoughts, and they become words. Control your words, and they become actions. Control your actions, and they become habits. Control your habits, and they become character. Control your character, and it becomes your destiny. And all of this evolves because of a single thought. Your thought. Control it and own it.

When you can perform a skill in your sport but have trouble executing it in competition, it's not a physical thing. It's a mental thing. Physically the athlete can do it. He has done it thousands of times. But mentally he's doubting himself or experiencing fear, which inhibits him from performing that skill during competition. Coaches must have pressure simulations in their practices to help their athletes. Players need to practice how they will play in competition. They need to maintain the right internal climate, no matter what the situation. I tell my players that the ideal internal temperature is between 86 and 88 degrees. Any less than 86 or any more than 88 is not good. They need to identify their ideal internal intensity level and must be able to summon that at any time.

In 2000, I had a player named Bucky Jencks, who was super talented in tennis, soccer, and track. Bucky was someone everyone liked, who always brought a healthy level of excitement with him. He had good character traits, but I felt I needed to help him contain his high energy level and channel it properly. In one regular season match at 'Iolani School, Bucky was playing doubles. Before the match started, he and his partner were feeling extremely confident that they would win, and win easily. He was overly excited and wanted badly to win the match without losing a single game. Well, Bucky and his partner won the first set, 6–0, but the second set was a much different story. They lost a game and Bucky began playing badly—I mean really badly. His internal temperature was well above the 88-degree mark, probably near the boiling point, and I would guess he hit triple digits in the second set. Bucky and his partner lost that set, and they came off the court for the ten-minute coaching break before the third set. Bucky's face was bright red, and he went on and on about how "lucky" his opponents had been to win the set. He kept this up until I said, "Bucky, quiet! I need you to stop talking and lie down on this bench!" He complied and I made sure everyone left him alone. I needed him to stay there, to breathe and relax for five minutes. I needed him to calm down and get his internal climate under control. After the five minutes, I gave him two strategic points to focus on. As he started to walk back onto the court, he paused by the gate and said, "Coach, that was brilliant coaching." I smiled, shaking my head, and he and his partner won the third set, 6–1.

Be Ready

An effective leader has total control of how his or her team is prepared. It's always better to be over prepared rather than under prepared. Great leaders have a habit of preparing so well that they know there's nothing more they can do. Vince Lombardi, the legendary head coach of the 1960s Green Bay Packers, was extremely detailed and meticulous in his preparation during football practices. He often told his team to "run it again," as he was convinced they would have an advantage over other teams if they were doing more than their competitors, if they worked harder and smarter. Coach Lombardi put his team through tough practices with great discipline because he believed that 99 percent of the work and training that goes into winning a Super Bowl happens during practices.

I believed the same thing. I would plan every tennis practice the night before, in order to be prepared and maximize our practice time. There were times when I told my team that we'd already won the championship, even before the state tournament began, because our preparation was so good. I wanted to give them confidence and a belief in themselves. I knew we were doing things that no other team was doing. I wanted them to have the feeling of deserving to win. We were ready and just needed to go out there and execute on court, trusting in ourselves and in our preparation.

Boxer Muhammad Ali said that 99 percent of the battle is won not when you're fighting but before you even step into the ring. He believed that a fight was won not in the ring, but in the time spent preparing for the boxing match. He said, "The fight is won or lost far away from witnesses—behind the lines, in the gym, and out there on the road, long before I dance under those lights." The Chinese general and philosopher Sun Tzu said, "Every battle is won before it is fought."

It is always better to be prepared and not have an opportunity, than to have an opportunity and not be prepared. The more prepared someone is, the luckier they tend to be.

It is true that luck is what happens when preparation meets opportunity. Many people perceive successful teams as being lucky sometimes. If and when luck does happen, it's because the leader takes a proactive approach in preparing the team for any possible opportunities. A great leader makes things look easy. But while he or she makes leading look easy, nothing of significance that you want to achieve ever comes easy. Great leaders spend countless hours preparing behind the scenes to make their team look refined and polished. Great leaders are consistent in making sure the team is well-prepared for anything and everything. 🎾

CHAPTER 7

KEY NO. 4:
COURAGE AND CONVICTION

"Courage doesn't mean you don't get afraid.
Courage means you don't let fear stop you."
—Bethany Hamilton

You will never cross the ocean unless you have the courage to lose sight of the shore. Great leaders have the courage to make tough, difficult decisions and will stand up and do the right thing at all times. They make these courageous decisions based on their values and principles and never compromise their belief in what they know is right. This is what great leaders do. Whether the situation appears simple or complex, great leaders always have the courage to make the best decisions based on integrity and ethics. This is often a test of the leader's character, which can either deepen the bond with the team or cause that bond to erode. Having the courage to do the right thing might not make everyone happy, but they will all respect you. They'll know where you stand, what kind of person you are, and what kind of team you want. Here's a quote I like to remember: "Standing alone doesn't mean I'm alone. It means I'm strong enough to handle things all by myself."

Own Your Decisions

It's very important to firmly establish your role as leader. When Vince Lombardi first became head coach of the Green Bay Packers, he immediately went to work defining the role of his players and his own role as head coach. Instead of putting the responsibility of winning on the players, he assumed that duty himself. He communicated to his team his expectations for their commitment and hard work during training, but he also outlined his own responsibilities in teaching and pushing them to maximize their potential. By taking on the burden of winning himself, Lombardi removed pressure from the players and allowed them to focus on being their best on the field. This also built trust between him and his team—that if both sides focused on their roles, they would be in the best possible position for success.

I made it a point to do this with my own teams. In jest, I told them that I would take all the blame—and all the glory— for whatever we did. Of course I said things like that to reduce the team's stress level and pressure to win. When we did win, I gave the credit to the players for their on-court performance, as well as to the other players who were watching, supporting, and cheering their teammates on from the sidelines. But I also assumed the responsibility when we lost—as the leader, it was my job to prepare the team to be successful. I didn't want my players to have to shoulder the blame for a loss. Instead I would assume there was something more I could have done, or something more I could have said to them before or during the game. Whatever the case, the leader takes full ownership of how the team performs.

In business or in sports, when there are problems and deficiencies with your team members, the problem is usually not them. It's usually you. Remember—everything starts with the leader. If there's dysfunction and low morale on your team, it's a reflection on you. Ineffective leaders will blame the team members. Great leaders will blame themselves, take responsibility, and find ways to solve the problem.

Risk Promotes Growth

Taking risks can be scary. It requires courage. If you're complacent and play it safe, you will never grow. As babies, we begin crawling and then take the risk to try and stand up on our own. Failure is falling. But we get up and try to stand again and again. Soon after we master standing on our own, we take the risk of walking. And then we take the risk of running. And then, sprinting. We've all taken these risks, otherwise we'd all still be crawling.

But when do we actually stop taking risks or become too scared to take them? Is it when we weigh the risk of succeeding versus failing? Sometimes people are complacent and resist change because they focus on what they have to give up, instead of what they have to gain. In order to grow, you need to take risks. The legendary investor Warren Buffet said, "Risk comes from not knowing what you're doing." Great leaders take calculated risks. They are educated and have the knowledge and courage to take calculated risks at the right times. Amazon's Jeff Bezos said, "Nine times out of ten, you're going to fail. But every once in a while, you'll hit a home run that in business terms is more like 1,000 runs. Given a ten percent chance of a 100 times payoff, you should take that bet every time."

Bezos also said, "Failure and invention are inseparable twins. To invent you have to experiment, and if you know in advance that it's going to work, it's not an experiment. If you're not stubborn, you'll give up on experiments soon. If you are not flexible, you will pound your head against the wall and you will not see a different solution to a problem you are trying to solve."

I began teaching private and group tennis lessons to Chris Iwamura when he was in the seventh grade at Punahou School. He already had great character traits and some good tennis ingredients in him. What I found even more impressive was that he was extremely coachable, super fun to work with, and had a constant striving for excellence. He wanted to be great. He was willing to take risks and try anything and everything to make his tennis game better. If there was a more effective way of doing things, he wanted to do it. I showed him more advanced stroke and footwork techniques and he did them. I showed him different strategies and various tactics and he did them. He was the opposite of complacent and an absolute joy to coach.

Chris was a strong singles player, but he had a big passion for doubles. He became one of the greatest doubles players I've ever coached. While on my boys' varsity team, Chris made it into the state doubles championship finals all four years. As a freshman, he won with Bucky Jencks. The next two years he won with another fine player, Nick Leong. And through these years he continued getting stronger and stronger because he had the courage to take risks in bettering his tennis game. As a senior, he partnered with a player named Matt Nakagawa. Both Matt and Chris were a little too risky with their serves, causing some unfortunate double faults on key points in the match. But I always admired Chris because he played to win rather than playing not to lose, and one of the main reasons for his success was his courage to take calculated risks.

Fast-forward to today: Chris's parents, owners of Honolulu's iconic Rainbow Drive-In, will be retiring soon and want Chris to take over. Remember I mentioned that Chris already possessed great character traits before I started training him in tennis? Well, that's because of his parents. He's now being groomed to take over management of Rainbow Drive-In, and his parents are having him learn every single facet of the business first. I've seen him working at every position in the restaurant, including cashier, cook, manager—even taking out the garbage. By learning every job, he is also earning the respect of the other employees. Because of his hands-on experience, they know Chris understands what they're thinking and feeling.

I'm so proud to have coached Chris and to have helped him learn life lessons on the tennis court. Having the courage to take calculated risks made Chris into the person he is today. I am confident that he will be a great manager and leader, and that all of his team members will be grateful to have him at the helm.

Be Honest

It takes courage to have open and honest communication with your team members. Honest feedback is extremely important. I always say that I don't give good feedback or bad feedback. I give honest feedback. This has helped me tremendously because during competition, when the pressure is on and my players look to me for coaching and guidance, my advice is very meaningful to them—because they know I'll be honest with them. "I know how you can win this match." I tell them. "If you do this and this, you will win." They believe me and trust me and try their best to execute that strategy.

In order to give honest feedback effectively, you need to understand your team members' personalities. There are so many different personality types. Not everyone can be coached in the same way. Not everyone can be communicated with in the same way. You need to know what triggers certain individuals and how to communicate with them effectively. I've had players that are extroverted and always very pumped up. Sometimes they're *too* pumped up, and I need to calm them down some so they can perform at their best. Other players who are introverted and mellow need to be pumped up for the opposite reason.

Having honest communication with your team members is important, because if you do it tactfully and make them realize you're trying to help them, they'll know that you care about them. It's best when you can give at least two compliments before offering constructive criticism. Not everyone enjoys receiving constructive criticism, but if communicated properly, it will be taken more as helpful feedback rather than criticism. Such feedback is viewed by team members in the context that you are helping them improve, rather than cutting them down. Following up with them is critical; it reinforces the importance of improvement in a particular area of concern. If your team member knows that it's important to you as the leader, then it becomes even more important to them.

Great leaders also provide an avenue for team members

to have open and honest communication with them. Communication works both ways, and great leaders take advantage of the fact that it's not a one-way street. It's good for team members to give the leader feedback. It helps give the leader insight into what team members are feeling and thinking. It helps the leader understand the pulse of the team. And it helps the team know that their opinions and feelings matter. This truly takes courage on the leader's part. Just as you might have constructive criticism for your team members, they will have constructive criticism for you. This open communication keeps you constantly in touch with the team's vibe. It also puts you on track toward building a "real" team, in which each member feels special because everyone is contributing and improving for the good of the team— including the leader. Just remember, a smart person knows what to say. A wise person knows whether or not to say it.

Make Everyone Matter

When I was in high school, I often practiced with some good friends on the Punahou School tennis team. When I met with them at Punahou's tennis complex, I was able to observe many of their varsity practices. I noticed that their team wasn't really a team. It was more like a group of individuals who were *sort of* on a team. They didn't seem to want to practice together, because they all appeared to have rivalries with one another. And when they did practice, they wouldn't give each other their best. And yet, they definitely would when they practiced with me. I also noticed that the team members were extremely divided, and that the "team" was severely fractured. Communication between team members was minimal; they just didn't look happy to be together.

When I became head coach in 1994, I wanted to make certain that we would have a "real" team on which everyone mattered and everyone was important. We would have open and honest communication in which team members could share their feelings with each other, and everyone realized that the team collectively was bigger than any of them individually. So during my first week of practice, I talked to the players about my observations of—and concerns about—past teams. I noted that in the past, a player wouldn't want to practice, or give it his best, with another player because they had a rivalry and often played each other in tournaments for ranking. The effect of this situation is counterproductive in a team environment, because it erodes the togetherness of the team and certainly doesn't help an individual develop his potential. I needed them to understand that the better one player gets, the better the other player gets, and vice versa. Helping each other be better individually helps the team collectively. It would take courage on their part to do this. Our focus would be the team, and how everyone could contribute to the team every single day, by trusting and helping each other.

And when, not if, an issue of concern arose, we would talk openly to resolve it. Many problems occur because people have misperceptions, miscommunication, misunderstandings, and misinformation. I told the boys that open and honest communication with each other is necessary in helping dispel negative feelings toward one another and helping the togetherness of our team. It's inevitable that we're going to play one another at times in tournaments. When we do, we go out there and respect each other, give our best effort, and are still friends again once the match is over, regardless of who wins or loses. And in terms of coaching, when we do play each other in singles or doubles, I will watch the match but not coach during the match. It's the fairest, cleanest way. They know each other very well and it avoids any possible coaching controversy, favoritism, or misperceptions.

I had seen early on, as a player, how important a coach can be to a team. In my youth, I played on a Hawai'i Youth Soccer Association team in the central O'ahu community of Mililani. Our team was comprised of all the top players from the American Youth Soccer Association teams in town. Our coach, Coach L., had great soccer knowledge and good experience as a coach and former player. Our practices were tough and we practiced specific skills and plays every day. Coach L. knew all our strengths and weaknesses and which positions we should play to give our team the best chance of winning. And win we did! We won a lot during two seasons with Coach L. But two months before the start of our third season, Coach L.'s work schedule changed and he could no longer coach our team. Mr. A. filled in and we lost every game we played. We had the same players on the team, the only difference being the new coach and his son added to the roster. Mr. A. didn't know how to practice us, nor which positions to play us in games, nor when to use substitutions. Moreover, although his son was the weakest player on our team, Mr. A. showed blatant favoritism by moving him into the starting lineup. Needless to say, we weren't having fun anymore and no longer looked forward to practices and games as we used to.

The following season, Coach L. returned and we were winning again, having fun and looking forward to every practice and game. We appreciated and respected Coach L. even more after our experience with Mr. A.

Please note that even though Mr. A. coached our third season, we called him Mr. A. instead of Coach A. He had authority over us but lost our respect from our very first practice. After seeing how impactful the coach really is to the team, I vowed to myself that if I ever became a coach, I would have the awareness, compassion, professionalism, and empathy to help lead my team the right way, to the best of my ability.

Embrace the Envy

When someone throws a brick at you, don't throw it back. Use it to build a house. I have witnessed many jealous people doing things that good people just don't do. Again, you have a choice in how you respond to such situations. It's a test of your character. A fool takes a knife and stabs people in the back. A wise man takes a knife, cuts the cord, and frees himself from the fools. I share this with you to urge you to have class and take the high road. Fools want to drag you down the dirt path and get you all muddy. Don't give them that satisfaction. Here's another bit of advice: Weak people seek revenge. Strong people forgive. Intelligent people ignore.

I have had countless students and players who achieved the number one state ranking, a state singles championship, a state doubles championship, and national rankings. But I am most proud of my impact in helping them become great people in society. Through the years, many of these players had told me about other players or other parents disrespecting them or saying mean things about them behind their backs. They couldn't understand why. I explained to them that because they were winning, accomplishing great things, and showing great character, others were envious of them. People have been envious of me too. But that's just how some people are. If we weren't winning, if we weren't doing anything of significance, why would anyone else care? They wouldn't. Envy happens when you're in the spotlight and achieving what others perceive as success. Knowing this, you have a choice to let them affect you or not. You can control how you respond. Embrace the envy. I would tell my players that I couldn't care less about what jealous people thought of me, because I didn't waste time thinking about them for even a minute. Don't let such people rent space on your internal hard drive. The next time someone talks behind your back or says something mean about you, take it as confirmation that you are doing something significant and are someone that they probably admire. If not, why would they spend time talking about you in the first place?

Because of my honest communication with my team, they know that I'm there to help them in any way possible. In a way, it makes them feel secure. Many players have told me that I'm more than a coach to them—I'm almost like a second father. What a compliment! 🎾

CHAPTER 8

KEY NO. 5:
YOU CREATE THE ENVIRONMENT

*"Helping one person might not change the world,
but it could change the world for one person."*
—Anonymous

Leaders are responsible for creating a team's "environment." But is that environment positive or negative? Is it good or bad? It's the leader who sets the tone in creating an atmosphere in which team members feel cared for, safe, excited, passionate, and productive in being able to flourish and accomplish the team's goals. You want your team members to feel like they belong. You want your team members to really love what they're doing and the people they're doing it with. You want them to feel there's nowhere else they'd rather be at the moment. You want them to feel a deep connection to the mission and the purpose of the team's goals, and to believe that everyone plays an important role in accomplishing these goals together.

The environment you create for your team directly helps the growth and success of each team member. For example, if you associate with people who get straight As in school, work hard, have high standards, and expect to accomplish great things, you'll likely start to have the same expectations for yourself. But what if you're hanging around people who are lazy, have no goals in life, or use drugs? Chances are you'll begin to go down that same road sooner or later. You're the same person, but now you're in a different environment with different influences.

In business, it is said that you need to take care of the people who take care of the customers. This is true. And often, if your business is quite large, you also need to take care of the people who take care of their people who take care of the customer. In sports, it's relatively similar if you replace *customer* with *result*. The head coach of a basketball team will want to take care of his assistant coaches, players, nutritionist, strength and conditioning coach, and administrative staff, in order to have a more favorable chance of getting the win. Everyone working together in a good, positive environment increases the probability for success in achieving the team's goals.

Listen First, Speak Last

One of the biggest communication problems is that we don't listen to understand. We listen to respond. Great leaders will listen carefully to what their team members are saying. By listening, you allow your team members to voice their opinions and share their concerns (whether privately or as a group), which helps their connection to and deepens their commitment to the team. This is critical. What you don't want is a team member who's unable to share his or her concerns. This can cause them to drift away until, sooner or later, their commitment to the team no longer exists. Listening takes time, but it allows you to read the pulse of your team. You get an immediate vibe on how they are feeling and they get a vibe on you as well. Listening is a skill. Most people in leadership positions have no problem talking, but many of them forget to listen.

More importantly, great leaders often speak last. They listen to the opinions of others first before they give their own. I remember something very interesting I heard the Dalai Lama say about listening: "When you talk, you are only repeating what you already know. But if you listen, you may learn something new." Speaking last ultimately helps you as the leader because you get to hear the opinions and views of others first. It helps others feel that they are being heard, and it helps you understand what they're thinking and feeling before you give your own feedback.

It's About People

Great leaders are genuinely interested in their team members. They want to help them in every possible way. They care deeply about their priorities and goals. It's similar to using your cell phone: When you're talking with someone in person, they can feel whether or not you really care about them. But if you're checking your cell phone at the same time, that person in front of you knows that your priority is phone first and him second. If you truly care about him, you'll set the phone on silent, even keep it out of sight, and really focus on and commit to the conversation at hand. This is hugely important because it makes it clear that he is your number one priority. The greatest gift you can give someone is your time. When you give someone your time, you're giving a portion of your life that you'll never get back.

Great leaders will always support their people. They will constantly ask their team members if they need anything. Team members will understand that what they're doing is important enough for you to be following up with them. This doesn't take much time to do, but the impact is huge—you're showing that you care about them and what they're doing. You definitely won't get the desired results or even come close to accomplishing your team's goals without focusing on your people. Pay attention to the well-being of your team members and you give yourself a chance to reach the goals you're striving for.

Most of us have heard the analogy about the importance of getting the right people on the bus. I like to use an airplane analogy. You need to get everyone on the plane in the right seats, in order to soar high above the clouds and reach your destination. The captain of an airliner has a copilot, a flight crew, and passengers. The leader needs to put everyone in the right role and in the right seat. By doing so, everyone on the plane knows that the leader cares about them because they're all in it together. Everyone's on the same plane, headed for the same destination, in a healthy environment, and every person is a reflection of the same high standards of excellence.

Give Everyone a Role

Personal growth leads to team growth. Do your job and accomplish the things you're responsible for doing. Everyone plays a crucial role in achieving the team's success. Every person wants and needs to feel valued and appreciated. It's the responsibility of the leader to make everyone on the team feel important. In order for team members to feel important and part of the team, the leader must clearly identify each person's role and how he or she can contribute toward making the team better. We have 12 players on the boys' varsity tennis team, I want the 12th player to feel just as important to the team as my number one player. For example, I tell the team that when we compete in the state championships, every match we win counts as one point towards the team championship point total, regardless of whether you're playing singles or doubles, regardless if you're our number one singles player or part of our number four doubles team.

At the beginning of the season, I speak individually with each player. I ask them to tell me what they think their strengths and weaknesses are. Their responses often surprise me, and they give me good insights into what they think of themselves. After listening to each player's self-assessment, I then share my own view of what he's good at and what needs improvement. I identify and focus on his strengths and explain that we need to keep practicing and building upon them—as well as working on his weaknesses. The players who made the team most likely did so because of their strengths.

One might have a strong forehand and serve. Another might have a good, solid all-court game. Yet another might have exceptional shot consistency and conditioning. Whatever the case, we need to identify it so the player knows what he's good at. This makes him feel good about himself, it creates a good learning environment for him, and he knows exactly how he can contribute to the team.

As head coach, I also have clearly defined roles for assistant coaches. The assistant coaches must share the same values and discipline as the head coach, which helps the cohesiveness of the team. The head coach might often exchange ideas with the assistant coaches, but the final decision always lies with the head coach. There will be difficult and challenging decisions to be made, but they must be made fairly and with integrity.

Tryouts, for example, must be handled fairly. Who will make the team? It's often easier in tennis because we have two players in a singles match—one who wins and one who loses. In golf, two players can play a round and the one with the lower score wins. In swimming and track, the athletes race, with a clear winner in each event. It can be more subjective in some team sports like baseball, football, basketball, and volleyball, which makes it more challenging. Every year in our tennis team tryouts, it seems to come down to 13 players competing to be on a 12-man team. I put myself in their shoes. Rather than the coach making a decision on which player he likes better, I feel the fairest way is to play a sudden death match. I know it's brutal, but it's fair. I know that if I were them, I wouldn't want the coach to make a judgement call on who makes the team. I would want to control my destiny and settle it on the tennis court.

The sudden death match has several benefits. First of all, the winner makes the team and earns instant respect from his teammates, since none of them would want to be in that pressure situation. Second, the winner instantly gets tougher and enjoys a big boost of confidence, knowing that he rose to the occasion and earned his spot on the team. Third, everyone feels bad for the player that lost, because anyone who plays sports knows how it feels to lose—especially when everyone is watching and keenly aware of the stakes. I always suggest that our team members go out of their way to give encouragement to the player who lost, when they see him the next day on campus. Fourth, players who lose the sudden death match often use the experience as motivation to be better. They bounce back by working harder and smarter, so that they can make the team the following year and avoid the sudden death match again.

As head coach, I also have clearly defined roles for parents, who want to help but need to be educated along the way, because the experience is not only new for their son or daughter, it's new to them too. The head coach needs to give them do's and don'ts. Once tryouts are completed, we have a meeting with all players and parents. We require at least one parent of every player to be present at this meeting, in which we go over the schedule and the upcoming season in general. This is when we define the parents' roles. Of course, we strongly encourage them to come and support the team at matches. Parents can also help provide food and drinks for the players after matches and can select a team parent to coordinate this. Parents are not coaches. Parents should not talk with coaches regarding lineups or playing times, because they need to understand there's a good reason for everything we do. Parents should schedule medical or dental appointments around the practice and match schedule. Parents should give the head coach advance notice of any trips or conflicts that may affect practices or matches. If there are other concerns, parents should feel free to contact the head coach directly. By clearly defining their role, the coach is able to better concentrate on guiding the team.

Protect Your People

Great leaders make their team members feel safe. Great leaders take care to protect their team members. The environment you create fosters this feeling of safety and caring. There have been countless times when I've walked out to the parking lot after a practice or game to find a player waiting to be picked up by a parent who is obviously late. When that happens, I always wait with him, even if it puts me behind schedule. It's the right thing to do. It's what I would want if I were in that player's tennis shoes, waiting under a dim light under cover of darkness, with no one else around. When your team members feel safe, they will communicate their concerns and vulnerabilities more freely. The bonds and relationships between leader and team members become greater and deeper. They will trust you and be loyal to you. (In business, developing such a trusting environment also encourages an employee to want to get to work and do their job, because they look forward to being there.) Having this kind of atmosphere prompts an athlete to get to practice and work hard because she looks forward to being there. She knows that you listen and that you care, and she feels safe because of the environment you've created. She feels that she's truly a part of a team and plays a key role in accomplishing the team's goals. This will eventually allow your team to accomplish extraordinary goals because, individually and collectively, they have a chance to perform up to their maximum potential.

The Bernard Gusman Story

I first met Bernard Gusman the summer after I graduated from high school, when I was asked to join the Junior Davis Cup training clinic at the Turtle Bay Resort on the North Shore of O'ahu. The top five players in the state in the boys and girls 18s and 16s division had been invited to this weekend event, and they all showed up. It was the best tennis clinic I've ever attended. Bernard had us doing drills and games that were very challenging but also super fun. We were working together, pushing each other hard, and helping one another. It was very competitive and cooperative. Bernard created a great, comfortable environment for us. The tennis training was so good that we were all quite sad when the weekend came to an end.

In 1992, four months after I joined Punahou as a tennis pro, Bernard was appointed the school's director of tennis. I was super excited that he would be the program's new leader as he possessed so much knowledge of the sport. I couldn't help but reflect back on that memorable tennis clinic he had conducted more than four years earlier. Much of the current staff was nervous about the personnel changes; nobody knew who would be kept on or let go. I quickly saw that Bernard had a high standard of excellence and great vision in developing the full potential of Punahou tennis. The school had eight courts and we developed programs for players of every age, at every ability level, in addition to our intermediate, junior varsity, and varsity tennis teams for boys and girls. It was absolutely impressive. There were a lot of moving pieces, but Bernard found a way to make everything work perfectly. He even started a kindergarten tennis program where all 150 kindergarteners were introduced to tennis. Little did we know at that time how important this program would be. We developed many players who started taking tennis in kindergarten and went on to be state singles and doubles champions and achieve number one state rankings.

Consequently, Punahou School tennis became one of the best, most respected programs in the United States. Many coaches and leaders from the mainland and other countries would come to Punahou to talk with Bernard and observe how we did what we did. They wanted to see how they might improve and enhance their own programs. This was a huge compliment to Bernard, but he would be the first to give all the credit to every member of our tennis staff. He was the leader with the vision who provided the guidance, and we were the ones who executed it on the tennis court every day.

The environment that Bernard created for us was extremely positive, and I looked forward to coming to work every day. He set a high standard for himself and for all of us to live up to, and he understood everything we were going through. Because we were at a school instead of a country club, the main focus was on the well-being of the students. He also attracted and put together one of the best tennis staffs for the care and training of the students. He introduced "pro training" twice a year, so that every staff member could share his or her best drills and games with one another. This kept things fresh and encouraged cooperation among our staff. He knew that each of us was a reflection of the others, and he wanted us to be the best we could be. He encouraged and supported every staff member to earn various tennis certifications and professional development. This added to each staffer's personal growth and also helped our team growth in the overall Punahou tennis program. Bernard knew all of our strengths and weaknesses and put us in the right roles to best help the students. He did not micromanage. He delegated and had confidence in us to get the job done.

There were many occasions when Bernard would get us together for a barbecue at his home, or to sing karaoke, for instance, which added to the cohesiveness and togetherness of our staff. We each felt that we were truly part of a team. It was special and it was fun. We all did our part to contribute in making Punahou tennis one of the best programs in the country. Our opinions and feedback mattered to Bernard. He cared about us. He had empathy. He paid attention to detail. He mentored us, which in turn helped us mentor younger, newer staff members. He created a healthy environment for everyone. Students loved to come hang out at the tennis court area to do homework and socialize with their friends. Parents enjoyed coming to pick up their sons and daughters and then staying longer to socialize with other families. It was amazing for me to see how impactful one person can be in creating such a positive atmosphere and affecting so many in a positive way. Bernard retired in 2016. In his retirement speech, he gave credit to his many staff members who'd helped and contributed to the success of Punahou tennis over the years. Today his legacy extends far beyond Punahou School to the many children and adults who enjoy playing tennis in Hawai'i. For these reasons, Bernard was the best director of tennis in the state of Hawai'i and one of the best in the United States. He was a great leader we respected—but more important, he became my friend. 🎾

CHAPTER 9

KEY NO. 6:
FIND YOUR PASSION

"The two most important days in your life are the day you were born and the day you find out why."
—Mark Twain

Passion can be defined as working hard for something you really love. Great leaders have love and passion for what they do. It may be work, but it doesn't really feel like it, because they simply love what they do and would probably do it for free. In turn, their team will feel this passion. Love and passion are necessary ingredients in inspiring and motivating team members. Inspiring others is the difference between a good leader and a great leader. Think about why you're in your current leadership position. Did you receive a company promotion that put you in a position to lead others? Were you an assistant coach who was promoted to head coach? Whatever the case, it is imperative that you have passion for what you're doing in order to help others. If you don't feel the passion, then find something else you can be passionate about and go do that. A leader needs to love and care about people. A leader needs to love interacting with people. A leader needs to love building relationships with people. You have to love what you do and genuinely love helping others. Passion leads to pursuing excellence, and excellence leads to inspiring belief in others to achieve goals they once thought impossible.

Strive for Excellence

Great leaders have high standards and strive constantly for excellence. You often hear the word *excellence*, but what does that really mean? Simply put, excellence can be defined as being the very best at something. I believe that before you start striving for excellence, you must start with the right mindset and attitude. In fact, I regularly challenge my teams to have not just a *good* attitude, but a superior attitude and a superior state of mind. There are many teams that have a good attitude and a good focus on what they're doing. I consistently remind my teams that we need to do our very best because if better is possible, then good is not enough. Striving for excellence is trying to be the very best you can be in every possible way, every single day. There's a difference between excellence and perfection. Perfection is unattainable, but if we chase perfection, we can catch excellence.

When you chase perfection, you tend to focus on paying attention to little details. These details are part of the process that helps you achieve the results you want. Such details must be attended to daily, whether you feel like it or not. We're all human and we face such dilemmas all the time. Say there's something that really needs doing, but you just don't feel like it—yet you find the discipline within yourself to go ahead and get it done anyway. Conversely, here's a similar dilemma: You know you shouldn't do something you really want to do, so somehow you find the self-discipline not to do it.

This is a major challenge I face with my players, and on a daily basis. There's a difference between a champion and finalist, I tell them. It's the difference between first place and second place, between winning and losing. Winners do things that losers don't like doing, because it takes sacrifice and commitment if you want to achieve anything significant. If something is important to you, you make your decisions accordingly, because you have a burning desire to accomplish it. Champions become champions because they settle for nothing less. They have a clear vision of what it takes to get there, and they focus and trust the process and do the right things all the time—whether they feel like it or not. They don't allow for distractions. If you believe it will work out, you'll see opportunities. If you believe it won't, you'll see obstacles. They have tunnel vision, and although they understand there will be obstacles along the way, they consistently make good choices in overcoming any obstacle they face. This is excellence. These actions become habits that you know you need to exercise in order to accomplish your goals.

Make People Believe

A great leader can make a good person great. She can make a great person greater. She can make an ordinary person extraordinary. And she can make an extraordinary person even more so. Successful leaders do this by inspiring belief in their team members. They want them to not only have dreams and goals, but also the belief in themselves to strive to achieve them. Records are made to be broken. A record performance shows you what was possible for someone else to achieve, because he believed he could do it. I like it when the bar is raised higher and higher, as it is in sports or business. This challenges others, including your competitors, to better themselves to keep up with your success. Remember that a high tide raises all boats.

The four-minute mile eluded champion runners for many years. John Landy, a highly exceptional athlete from Australia, ran the mile in 4:02 on seven different occasions. In January 1954, Landy said, "Frankly, I think the four-minute mile is beyond my capabilities. Two seconds may not sound much, but to me it's like trying to break through a brick wall. Someone may achieve the four-minute mile the world is wanting so desperately, but I don't think I can." On May 6, 1954, on a windy, rainy day at Oxford University, Roger Bannister broke the four-minute mile with a time of 3:59.4. Bannister, an athlete from the United Kingdom, was contemplating not running that day because of unfavorable weather conditions. But his coach believed in Bannister and said to him, "I think you can run a 3:56 mile. If you have a chance and don't take it, you may regret it for the rest of your life." Then, 46 days later, John Landy broke the four-minute mile with a time of 3:58. Since then, the mile record has been lowered by almost 17 seconds. Once Bannister did it, Landy began to believe that it could be accomplished. Belief in yourself is so powerful and inspiring to others that it can turn dreams into reality. It can turn the impossible into the possible. The impossible is what nobody can do until somebody does it. Think of the many other nearly impossible things we see in life that could very well become possible.

Boxer Muhammad Ali famously said, "I am the greatest. I said that even before I knew I was." As a leader, I know that belief can be extremely powerful, but then so can doubt. You need to consistently inspire belief in your team members to focus on what they want to achieve, and on what you want the team to achieve together. But they must know you really mean it. You, as the leader, must believe it too.

The celebrated San Francisco 49ers quarterback Joe Montana said, "Winners imagine their dreams first. They want it with all their heart and expect it to come true. There's no other way to live." His coach, Bill Walsh, said, "Joe Montana came to the San Francisco 49ers believing he was extraordinary. My job was to convince him that he was beyond extraordinary."

And then there's Robert Kraft, owner of the New England Patriots, recalling the first time he met quarterback Tom Brady, during Brady's second season in the National Football League. "He came down to training camp and introduced himself," Kraft said. "Here was this skinny beanpole, with this pizza under his arm. He says, 'I'm Tom Brady.'"

"I know who you are," Kraft told Brady. "You're our sixth round pick."

"I'm the best decision this organization has ever made," Brady responded.

"Normally, that kind of bravado would be a turn off,"

Kraft later recalled. "I don't know how to explain it, but with him it resonated."

Most of us are aware of how Nike's Phil Knight revolutionized the athletic footwear industry. Geoff Hollister was a small town Oregon farm boy who was a runner at the University of Oregon for coach Bill Bowerman and later became Nike's third employee. Geoff provided further insight into the Nike saga in his book, *Out of Nowhere: The Inside Story of How Nike Marketed the Culture of Running.*

"I have thought often of what it all means," he wrote. "Life thrusts you into a competitive environment. How do you prepare for the realities and the unknown? Hopefully you have a mentor, a Bowerman, who pushes you at that critical time. A time when someone has a belief in your future more than you do. It's not about how long you live but how you contribute. It's about doing your best and doing the right things. It's about recovering from your mistakes and not giving up. It's about the baton pass to a new generation. It's about the realization that you cannot go it alone. It takes a team. In the end, you are somewhere in the middle, part of a never-ending process. The future will never remember what was in your bank account or what kind of car you drove. The future will remember that wild ride of life where you believed in others and left a gift behind for someone else to dream the impossible. The gift was your own life. It does not matter whether it was long or short. What did you leave behind?"

Relentless Pursuit of Success

All great leaders and successful teams are driven to succeed. If you're merely interested in something, you'll do what's convenient. If you have a major commitment, you'll do whatever it takes to succeed. You must have a relentless drive to achieve both small goals and big ones. It's true that if something is important to you, you will find a way. If it's not, you will find an excuse. Elon Musk, owner and CEO of Tesla, said, "If other people are putting in 40-hour work weeks and you're putting in 120-hour work weeks, you will accomplish in four months what will take others one year to do." Many things in life aren't fair or equal, but everyone gets the same 24 hours a day, seven days a week. And did you know that there are 1,440 minutes in one day? The grass is not always greener on the other side. It's greener where you water it. We make time for what we really want.

In order to have this relentless drive to succeed, you must be comfortable in uncomfortable situations. You must be able to tolerate challenging and often unfavorable circumstances. For example, if you and I are in a swimming pool, what happens if I challenge you to see who can hold his breath longer under water? Now, I assume that you are competitive and want to win. So you accept the challenge and we both go under. After 45 seconds or so, what do you do when you begin to feel uncomfortable? Obviously, you come up for air. Now, I might be feeling just as uncomfortable as you at that moment, but I really want to win. So I'll stay under water a little longer and tolerate it. If you really want to win at something, you often must tolerate the discomfort. Leaders and team members who are driven to succeed will be determined to put up with a little extra when dealing with uncomfortable situations.

In a presentation I saw by actor and filmmaker Denzel Washington, he said, "Don't just aspire to make a living. Aspire to make a difference. Anything you want good, you can have. So claim it. Work hard to get it. When you get it, reach back. Pull someone else up. Each one, teach one. Just because you're doing a lot more doesn't mean you're getting a lot more done. Don't confuse movement with progress. So have dreams, but have goals. Life goals. Yearly goals. Monthly goals. Daily goals. And understand that to achieve these goals, you must apply discipline and consistency. In order to accomplish your goals, you must apply discipline and consistency every day. Not just on Tuesday and miss a few days. You have to work at it. Every day you have to plan. You've heard the saying we don't plan to fail, we fail to plan. Hard work works. Working really hard is what successful people do."

The Ikaika Jobe Story

I first met Ikaika Jobe when he was ten years old and I began training him in our Rising Stars tennis program at Punahou. I recognized immediately that he was a talented athlete with a great passion for tennis. Ikaika loved the sport and loved to compete against his peers. His strengths were his footwork, strokes, understanding of the game, and instincts with his shots. His weakness was his attitude and lack of discipline. And by that I mean he had a bad attitude and very little discipline, and it was clear to me that this is what would keep him from developing his full potential in tennis.

Far too often when he lost points or games, he reacted by throwing his racket, slamming a tennis ball into the fence, or using unacceptable language. Yes, I know—he was violating my rule on no racket, ball, or verbal abuse. I always looked forward to seeing and helping Ikaika in our group training, but I also needed to contain his actions. There were other nine-, ten-, and eleven-year-olds in the program, and I needed to do this quickly, to help put him on the right path and also to maintain the respect and control of the others. So I warned Ikaika in front of his peers that the next time he violated any one of the abuses, he would force me to give him a time-out.

Not more than ten minutes later, he lost a game and slammed a ball into the back fence. True to my word, I announced, "Ikaika has given himself a time-out because of the abuse violation and will sit and watch in the shaded area and will not participate in the next two games." He was shocked. It appeared to me that I was the first coach to ever give him any real discipline or consequences for his actions. Keep in mind that Ikaika has a great passion for tennis, and it was killing him to have to sit and watch while the others continued having fun in our training. After 15 minutes, I had him rejoin the group, and his attitude was much improved. In fact, he was fine for the rest of our session. He had been embarrassed but also, I hoped, impacted in a positive way.

But in our next training session, the outbursts happened

again, and so the 15-minute time-outs continued. I knew that Ikaika was trying not to react inappropriately, but he just couldn't help himself. He had been this way for so long. I really liked that he was trying, but a violation is a violation, and he needed this type of discipline to help him in tennis and as a person. Slowly he learned to control himself better, until one training session when he was having a really bad day. He lost a game within the first ten minutes of training and threw his racket, nearly hitting another player.

"Ikaika, get out!" I yelled. "You can get off the court, close the gate, and watch the rest of our training from outside." He looked frightened, but I knew I needed to shake him up.

I continued to help Ikaika for two years in Rising Stars, and slowly his self-discipline improved, which also greatly helped his tennis. Soon after, his father hired a private coach to train his son, and this coach convinced his father to discontinue training at Punahou and train only with him. I would see Ikaika at junior tournaments because many of my players were competing as well. Ikaika is an extremely likable person and his tennis game was improving mainly because of his talent. But how much could he improve? Could he develop correctly and reach his full potential—physically, mentally, and emotionally? As I observed him in tournaments over the next few years, I noticed that the improvement we had made with his discipline was fading away.

Then, when he was in the ninth grade, Ikaika tried out for Punahou boys' varsity and made the team with no problem at all. It was as if he was yearning for the discipline he knew our team stressed, and he began absorbing everything like a sponge. Ikaika was a strong freshman player and I knew he would make an impact at the state championship. I had missed not being able to help in his development during the past few years, and I felt he had missed me too. He really loved being on the varsity and was a great team player. As a singles player he finished number three in the state championship.

The following year, he won the state singles championship as a sophomore but even more important, his attitude and discipline improved tremendously, which gave him better results with his tennis. Before tryouts during his junior year, his father requested a meeting with me. The meeting also included my assistant coach, Ikaika's new private coach, and Ikaika himself. It was clear to me that his father had Ikaika's best interest at heart and was trying to make the best decisions for his son. It was also clear that his new private coach had only a vague basic understanding of tennis, and yet was representing himself as someone with advanced intelligence in the sport. The problem was that Ikaika's father believed everything he said—for example, that Ikaika was going to be the next Andre Agassi.

In our meeting, the private coach asked me if I'd allow him to observe Ikaika in our team practices. "Absolutely not," I told him. Now I began to understand what this meeting was really about. Because Ikaika was going to be "the next Agassi," they were debating whether he should even be playing on our team. I asked Ikaika what he wanted, and he said he wanted to play varsity tennis. But apparently his father and private coach had already decided that he would instead train for the professional tour. I could see the huge disappointment in his eyes, because he knew how much varsity tennis helped him. He knew how much he needed us and loved playing on varsity.

Throughout that year, the private coach overtrained and overworked him, apparently without any understanding of the importance of rest and recovery. Needless to say, Ikaika was injured. It was a bad shoulder injury that kept him from making serves or overheads. Of course this was a major setback and soon after, his father terminated the arrangement with the private coach. But the damage had been done. Ikaika then asked me for private lessons during his senior year and told me he was returning to play varsity tennis. The problem was that he was broken—the shoulder injury was still an issue, and I was supposed to help put the pieces back together. So we trained and practiced shots that he could make, while avoiding others that caused him pain. During the regular season, I let him play in matches only if he served underhand and didn't hit any overhead shots, so that his shoulder could continue to heal. He agreed. Everyone expected Ikaika to win the state singles championship as a senior, especially because he had already won as a sophomore. But no one outside of our team really understood his true condition. For his part, Ikaika didn't expect to win states—he just wanted to be healthy and play tennis with no pain. I knew this was a good mindset for him, because he wasn't putting pressure on himself to win (although everyone else was). I felt some of the pressure myself, as everyone knew I was training Ikaika privately. If he didn't win, some would undoubtedly lay the blame at my feet. But in fact, that would be fine with me; all I wanted was to focus and give my best to every player on my team.

Ikaika did play his way into the state singles championship final. By this time, he could serve with regular form again, although he couldn't serve hard or with much power. His serves were actually quite soft and would definitely favor the other finalist. During the first set, his opponent played very smart and very well and made Ikaika look like his punching bag. I fully understood what Ikaika was feeling and thinking. I could see he was letting all the pressure and high expectations get to him, and this was affecting his performance. He wasn't even hitting his forehand as he usually did. He lost the first set, and I walked onto the court during the coaching break.

"Ikaika, you look like a punching bag out there!" I said. "You need to start throwing your own punches. You have the best and biggest forehand in the state, but you haven't hit it once. If you're going down, if you're going to lose, then at least hit all the shots that you have in your arsenal. Hit all the shots we've practiced and hit that forehand as many times as possible."

Ikaika went out for the second set and did just as we'd discussed. He looked like a different person out there. He looked like a champion. He won the second set and we talked again during the coaching break before the third and deciding set. I told him how proud I was of him. I told him I was most proud of his attitude and discipline, and I reminded him about the time I'd kicked him out of Rising Stars and made him watch the rest of the training from outside the gate. We both laughed. I told Ikaika to continue hitting and trusting his forehand, and I reminded him to attack the net when his opponent was on defense. Well, he went out there and did exactly that. (I do love it when my players actually listen and do the things we talk about!) Ikaika won that third set and earned his second state singles championship. He represented our team and our school with class. Everyone could see the passion that he had for tennis, and I was happy to have helped guide him in the right direction.

After graduating from high school in 2001, Ikaika played college tennis at Saint Louis University for three years and at Boise State University in his senior year. He went on to play professionally and achieved a world ranking that placed him in the top 50 in the country. I strongly believe that if Ikaika had continued training at Punahou, instead of leaving after Rising Stars, and had had the right private coach to mentor him, he could have fully developed his potential and reached an even higher level—much higher. Instead, he was virtually undisciplined for four years before coming back under the Punahou umbrella for varsity, and then suffered that serious injury during his junior year. Still, all things considered, Ikaika had a pretty good tennis career.

But the story isn't finished yet. He also went to law school, and while he was a practicing attorney, he also served for three years as head coach for Punahou's girls' varsity tennis team. And when I retired as head coach of the boys' varsity, I recommended Ikaika to succeed me. He has now held this position for two years. (He tells me that he likes law, but he loves tennis!) Even better, Ikaika was then named Punahou School's director of tennis, leaving his law firm for this new and exciting challenge.

Building other great leaders is so very rewarding. I am so proud to have helped develop and mentor Ikaika Jobe. I am confident that he will do the same in sharing his passion for tennis with all the students and staff at Punahou, and that he will ultimately build and mentor other future leaders. 🎾

CHAPTER 10

KEY NO. 7:
WELCOME ADVERSITY

*"Life is not about waiting for the storm to pass.
It's about learning to dance in the rain."*
—Vivian Greene

We all experience stress and adversity in our lives. Let me predict the future for you right now. You will continue to experience stress and adversity in your life. Your team will experience these challenges, and so will your children. Of course, stress and adversity are inevitable. However, we shouldn't be trying to protect either our team or our children from such challenges. Instead, we should be teaching them how to face them. We need to have the right perspective in viewing adversity as a challenge to overcome, rather than a problem to worry about. Life doesn't get easier. You need to get stronger. In order to be stronger, we need to know that when stress and tough situations happen, we're prepared to deal with them properly. A great leader expects the unexpected and teaches and prepares his or her team accordingly.

When you and your team experience adversity, you become stronger and tougher because you dealt with it and got through it. You were tested and you're a better person for having gone through that test. Being fearful or trying to avoid adversity won't prepare you for when it inevitably happens. This is one of the reasons why some people crack and choke under pressure. They aren't prepared for the bad times and are hoping they won't happen to them. But inevitably, they will. The best leaders in sports and business have trained their teams to be prepared, and to expect and even welcome these challenging situations. They can look forward to new challenges, knowing they'll be stronger for the experience.

Be Resilient

Did you know that Abraham Lincoln lost eight elections, failed twice in business ventures, and had a nervous breakdown before he became president of the United States? Each of us has lost at something, has failed at one time or another. We've all heard the saying that when you get knocked down, you need to get right back up. It's called resiliency, and all great teams have it. All great leaders have it. They are able to consistently bounce back from disappointment. This is why they succeed. There are always highs and lows in life, and you have the choice to get back up from every "low," from being knocked down, from losing, from being disappointed— or you can choose to stay down. This choice is critical and is something you control completely.

Defeat is a temporary condition. Giving up is what makes it permanent. Bruce Lee said, "Defeat is a state of mind. No one is ever defeated until defeat has been accepted as a reality." He also said, "Do not pray for an easy life. Pray for the strength to endure a difficult one."

Being resilient is a choice. It's easy to punch, but can you also take punches? I liked hearing Sylvester Stallone say, in one of his Rocky movies, "Life isn't about how hard you can hit, but how much you can get hit and still keep moving forward." Challenges are going to happen to you and your team. I guarantee it. You'll win some and you'll lose some. One of my favorite quotes, which I like to use when my players get beaten in a match, is from Confucius, who said, "Our greatest glory is not in never falling, but in rising every time we fall."

Perform Under Pressure

Stress and adversity definitely build character. They are also a test of character. We shouldn't protect our team members from challenging and uncomfortable situations. We need to teach them how to deal with them and explain why that's important. But it's how you respond with resiliency that makes all the difference. How you respond impacts everyone around you. I love watching players and teams in competition when their backs are up against the wall; seeing how they respond truly reveals their character. I like watching a team that's a huge underdog compete and rise to the occasion. I like watching a team that's heavily favored and under major pressure to win, and witnessing their great attitude, poise, and discipline shine through, regardless of the score or whatever struggle they're dealing with.

The 2017 Super Bowl was a great example of this. The Atlanta Falcons were way ahead of the New England Patriots, by a score of 28–3. But then millions of people witnessed an unprecedented comeback by Tom Brady and his teammates that resulted in a 34–28 overtime victory. What I found most impressive when the Patriots were losing was that they never appeared to turn against one another. Nobody placed any blame on anyone else because of the hole they found themselves in. Not one Patriot player looked negative or dejected. They just kept competing, one play at a time. If you have discipline, that's all you can do, and that's what you expect from your teammates as well. Head coach Bill Belichick, as their leader, has instilled this discipline in his team. They can handle adversity. In fact, it challenges them. It brings out the very best in them. They seem to expect it and thrive on it. This is what champions do.

Every person experiences setbacks, disappointments, and losses. Team members need to view these things as opportunities to better themselves, rather than feeling frustrated and discouraged. Frustration is the easy response. It's what average people do. Champions don't do this. Champions know they have a choice in how they respond to adversity. It's all about having the right perspective. You need to remember that stress and adversity are like a rainstorm. The skies might be dark and gloomy, it might rain buckets today and tomorrow, but it won't rain every day for the rest of your life. The sun will eventually come out again and you'll see blue skies. Champions always have the right perspective to motivate themselves to be better for the next challenge. It's an opportunity for them to make themselves stronger and tougher, which not only helps them in sports, but it prepares them for life's greater challenges.

Excited vs. Nervous

In sports, every athlete experiences pressure during competition. Some athletes thrive on pressure and others don't. But pressure in competition is inevitable and coaches must prepare their players for it. There are basically two responses to pressure. One is when players allow fear to consume them, become overly nervous, and choke. The other is what we will focus on. I make my players understand they should be excited when they feel pressure, because it means they're doing something significant. They're doing something special. They have a real opportunity in front of them. A coach must train players to have the correct perspective on pressure. When players are asked how they feel before a competition, they often reply that they're nervous. But the coach must convince them that they're excited, not nervous. Feeling excited is clearly the better response. They must look at it as a challenge to overcome rather than a problem to worry about. Pressure can be a test of your players' toughness, an excellent indicator of where they stand in their overall development. The more pressure situations they experience, the tougher and stronger they become. It ultimately becomes a test of their character. Many coaches build physical skills in their athletes, but they also need to build internal mental skills.

They need to develop mental toughness. We hear it a lot, but what exactly is mental toughness? It's the ability to create and maintain the right kind of internal feeling regardless of the circumstances. In order to win a championship or consecutive championships, players need to have that mental toughness—a positive perspective in dealing with, and even looking forward to, pressure.

And then there's stress. Stress is a good thing. It helps you grow to be a stronger person. Great leaders train their teams to get comfortable in uncomfortable situations. I coach my players by identifying two types of stress: necessary and unnecessary. Necessary stress is fine; unnecessary stress is not. This is very simple for me to explain, and it's very important to keep things as simple as possible when communicating with your players. Players who worry about things they cannot control experience unnecessary stress. At the middle or high school level, they might be worried about an upcoming math test while they're in the middle of soccer practice. During a basketball game, they might be preoccupied with a science project that's due in two days. Nevertheless, they need to focus on the task at hand and not worry about something that they can't do anything about at that moment.

Necessary stress involves dealing with situations that players can control. An athlete might have a deadline for submitting college applications, and the stress might be related to their time management. Another athlete might experience stress in studying for multiple final exams. These stressful situations are necessary and we've all experienced them. As coaches, we need to make certain that our players focus only on things they can control. Otherwise, they can become mentally and physically fatigued, stressing out unnecessarily over things they can't control.

The Will Grosswendt Story

The fact is, most athletes do put pressure on themselves unnecessarily. A player's view of a pressure situation can be magnified, which then leads to performance below capability.

In 2005, a senior named Will Grosswendt played third doubles on my team. He was a talented athlete and a good tennis player. He had delightful parents and was a very nice boy himself. As we finished our regular season and our qualifying tournament for the state championship, I received a phone call from Will's mom. She informed me that Will was feeling so much pressure to win that he was underperforming in matches, even though he and his partner had qualified to participate in the state tournament. It was true. Will looked great in practice and even in practice matches. But when he played in the qualifying tournament, he seemed really shaky and uncertain with his shots. His play was inconsistent. Will's mom believed he felt so much pressure to win because of our long championship streak, and that he didn't want to let me or his teammates down. I told her I'd talk with him privately.

The next day, as I prepared the courts for practice, Will arrived with his rackets in hand. I took him aside and said, "I got a phone call from your mom, Will. She says you're feeling lots of pressure, and it's affecting your performance in the matches."

"I feel tons of pressure to win, Coach," he replied, "so much pressure. My shoulders feel tight all the time, and I don't play nearly as good in matches as I do in practice."

"But why is that?" I asked. "The only player who should feel that kind of pressure is a number one ranked player or a defending singles or doubles champion. Are you ranked number one in the state? Are you the defending state singles champion? Or the defending state doubles champion?"

"No," he allowed.

"So you really shouldn't feel any pressure," I pointed out, "because you haven't really achieved anything significant yet!"

He thought about that for a moment and then said, "Coach, you're right!"

Soon we were both jumping up and down and repeating in unison, "You don't have any pressure because you haven't achieved anything yet!" I could almost see the tightness in his shoulders melt away and his head become clearer. Now he could relax and play tennis with the mindset he needed to win matches, rather than obsessing about what he had to lose. He now understood that he had nothing to lose and everything to gain.

When the state championship doubles tournament began a week later, I could see from the first match that Will had something to prove to himself. He was having fun, finally playing up to the potential he had shown in practice. After winning their first two matches, he and his partner competed in the quarterfinals against his teammates, a pair that was our number one doubles team and also the number one seed in the tournament. When our team members play each other in a tournament, I don't coach either team during the match. It's the fairest way to do it. Instead I give all four players feedback when the match is over. It avoids misperceptions and keeps things clean.

Will and his partner had a focus and a drive that was getting stronger with every set they played. They defeated their teammates and found themselves in the semifinals, which they dominated. Their consistency and confidence continued to grow, and they soon found themselves on stadium court playing for the state doubles championship. Win or lose, I felt so proud of Will. He had exhibited good character from the first time I met him, and he continued to develop this character throughout high school. Our team's discipline and pursuit of excellence helped Will flourish even more as an individual. He was a great guy who was representing his school, team, and family at the highest level. And now he was unlocking his true potential in tennis with an opportunity to earn a state doubles title.

There was no denying him that day. He and his partner won the match, and Will finished his senior year and his high school tennis career as a state doubles champion. He had definitely overcome the odds—as a freshman he had barely made the junior varsity team and was ranked last on the JV roster. Then he went from being a varsity senior playing third doubles in the regular season to winning the state championship.

Pressure can clearly play some weird tricks on people's minds. Accordingly, we must consistently help our team members *welcome* stress, viewing it as a challenge to overcome, and making sure they don't bring any more unnecessary stress upon themselves. 🎾

CHAPTER 11

KEY NO. 8:
REAL WINNING OCCURS WITHIN

*"You never really play an opponent. You are playing
yourself and your own highest standards."*
—Arthur Ashe

What does success really mean? When does someone become successful? What is success versus winning? Is there a difference between losing and getting beaten? These are all important questions. Every great leader needs to have his team strive for real winning and real success. A great example of "real" winning is when my team keeps playing as hard as they can, even when they realize they might lose the match.

Success is a Journey

Success can only be measured after a long period of time. You don't achieve success tomorrow or next week. It's not a short-term thing. It takes time to know whether or not you were truly successful. You might "win" by gaining a new client, making a sale, or winning a game, but does this one victory make you successful? The answer is no. Achieving success is done day by day. You need to better yourself every day. You need to learn something every day. After all, you don't go to the gym and work out for ten hours one day to get in shape. You get in shape and improve your fitness by working on it every day. It's something you need to do consistently.

A river cuts through rock not because of its power, but because of its persistence. Champions do things every day to make sure they are moving in the right direction. Franklin D. Roosevelt said, "There are many ways of going forward, but only one way of standing still." Hoping and praying for victory and success is fine, but deserving it is what really matters. Great leaders and great teams persevere and eventually achieve success. A great leader never says she'll do it tomorrow because she knows that tomorrow she'll wish she'd started it today. Babe Ruth said, "It's hard to beat someone who never gives up." Persistence becomes a habit if you have a burning desire for success.

Losing vs. Getting Beaten

There's a big difference between losing and getting beaten. Losing is what happens when you have a poor attitude or give poor effort that leads to a loss. Getting beaten is when you had a great attitude and gave great effort, but still came out on the short end just because your opponent was better that day. There have been times when my tennis players won their matches with a poor attitude and maybe a 70 percent effort that was just enough to win. Needless to say, this is when I would gather them together for some honest communication. I would share with the team how disappointed and embarrassed I was watching their performance. That singles player or doubles pair was representing our team, our school, me and and their parents, and they should have exhibited their best attitude and their best effort. It's not a switch that you turn on and off.

If anything, the switch should be on all the time. It's about giving your best from the first point until match point.

It's about competing and playing with class all the time. There have been many times when a player on my team would have a great attitude and give it everything, and still get beaten. Again I'd gather the team together for a talk. I'd share with them how proud I was watching that player's performance, and how he represented our team, our school, myself and his parents in the best possible way—with ultimate class. One benefit of these little post-match talks was that my team really understood what I was about and what we should be striving for. It definitely wasn't about winning. It was how we competed. It was about our attitude and effort. It was about having good character and giving our best. It was about having fun and enjoying the experience. This is real winning.

Most if not all of my players told me in one way or another that they appreciated my effort and dedication as their coach. Some of our athletes may have taken the things we did for granted, only because they hadn't previously had team experiences with any other coaches. But many of my players who went on to play college tennis expected their new coaches to be equal, if not better. The fact is, I believe the majority of them were extremely frustrated with their college tennis experiences, because their new coaches were nowhere close to the standards they expected. Maybe the new coach didn't care as much, didn't have enough expertise, or simply treated his players unfairly. This is when our players recognize and truly appreciate the priceless experience they had in high school varsity tennis. And this is when I received phone calls from many of them, thanking me for teaching them important life lessons while they were learning to play better tennis. I love when those players tell me how valuable and enjoyable their experience had been, years and even decades after they graduated. I continue to have regular reunions with many of my alumni players, who reminisce about what they believe to be priceless experiences.

Little Victories Lead to Big Ones

It's crucial to strive for little victories. Small wins lead to big successes. The little things matter. As an example, one little difference that can make a huge difference is attitude— positive or negative. A bad attitude is like a flat tire. You can't go anywhere until you change it. The same thing applies to your mood. A bad mood is a reflection of your attitude. Change your attitude and you'll change your mood.

You, as the leader, should give hope to your team. In tennis, some players see only the clouds and stormy skies of a match. Champions see the sun peeking through. Getting through this match and focusing on the positives might give your team a little victory that could very well lead to a bigger one. Having hope and envisioning what might be possible is a powerful thing. Martin Luther King Jr. said, "If I cannot do great things, I can do small things in a great way."

Getting through a little challenge can help your team deal with bigger challenges later. Make your team understand that one small crack doesn't mean that you are broken. It just means you were put to the test and didn't fall apart. Life does not get easier. You just get stronger. Never be ashamed of the scars that life inflicts. A scar means the hurt is over, the wound is closed, you endured the pain, and you've moved on as a stronger person.

How can you have a little victory if you don't try? Don't worry about failure. Worry about the chances and opportunities you miss when you don't try. Tony Robbins said, "No matter how many mistakes you make or how slow you progress, you're still way ahead of everyone who isn't trying." Great leaders encourage their teams to strive for goals beyond their reach. They want them to try for things the team originally thought was impossible. No matter what level your team may be, always encourage them to strive for those little victories.

The Brandon Lee Story

In 2009, a ninth grader named Brandon Lee signed up for tryouts for my team. Ultimately, Brandon would become one of our best stories, because he exemplified what I believe real winning and real success are, which in turn reinforced our whole team's standard of excellence.

Before tryouts began, I kept hearing from numerous players and parents about Brandon's attitude and behavior in tournaments, which was the opposite of what our team was striving for. They all said that he was a very talented tennis player but his attitude and behavior were very bad—in fact, on the opposite end of the good-bad spectrum. So they were very curious about whether Brandon would actually make the team. I told all of them that I hadn't seen Brandon play and that I wouldn't prejudge anyone. He would go through tryouts like every other player, and I would observe him the same as anyone else.

In fact, I was very impressed with Brandon because he was so talented and because his attitude and behavior in tryouts were so good. Brandon made the team as a freshman. I believed he could help our team best that year by playing doubles, and he had a very good regular season. I saw no signs of any bad behavior during the season, and it appeared that Brandon really enjoyed being part of a team—rather than playing individually as he had before.

In our post-season qualifying tournament, Brandon and a partner were up against a very good doubles team from 'Iolani School, competing for third and fourth place. The match was very exciting because all four players competed well, and it went to a third-set tiebreaker. The tiebreaker was also very thrilling, but the other team beat us. After losing match point, Brandon walked toward the net to shake hands with his opponents. On his way to the net, he threw his racket to the side of the court near his tennis bag. It wasn't a hard, angry throw, but it was a throw nonetheless. As he and his partner exited the court in obvious disappointment, I took Brandon aside. I told him I was very proud of how he competed during the match, but that throwing the racket was unacceptable. It was his only flaw, but it violated our team rules. He acknowledged this and did his 100 push-ups right there on the walkway, just outside of the tennis court in front of all the spectators and competitors. Some of these onlookers thought Brandon was doing push-ups because he'd lost the match! I set them straight. It was the first time I saw him exhibit behavior that was unacceptable, and it needed to be immediately addressed.

When the season was over, Brandon continued to play for his personal ranking. But I saw a different Brandon in these tournaments, exhibiting behavior that included racket, ball, and verbal abuse, visible frustrations, and strong negativity. It wasn't a pleasant sight, and it definitely didn't help him compete to the best of his ability. I began working with him in private and group tennis lessons, challenging him to do only things that would help him win. Once we identified and isolated the counterproductive behavior, he truly began to realize how high my standards were for him and for our team. Brandon began to understand that he needed to control his hands and mouth in order to control his thoughts and his destiny in tennis matches. Because he'd had a serious lack of discipline in his training prior to joining our team, I told him that it would be a process that would take time and lots of consistent reinforcement. I warned him that we would have some flare-ups along the way. But this was the only way he could change those bad habits into good ones, and truly unlock his athletic potential in tennis and add to his fun and fulfillment when competing. Brandon worked really hard and was committed to achieving this high standard for himself during his high school career.

Fast-forward to 2012, and Brandon was team captain—a senior playing singles and seeded number one at the state singles championship tournament. Seeded second was an extremely talented eleventh grader from Kamehameha Schools who Brandon had beaten twice during the season. Now they found each other on opposite ends of the tennis court again, this time playing for the state singles title. Brandon was well-prepared and confident going into the match, which took place in front of a huge crowd of spectators, many of whom hadn't seen Brandon play in years.

Brandon executed his shots and strategy very well and won the first set. I coached him during the 90-second break between sets. I told him he needed to continue to execute this strategy, but also to realize that his opponent was a great competitor and was definitely going to raise his level of play in the next set. He needed to do the same. During the second set, they each won many grinding, grueling points, and the level of play was very high. His opponent took that set with incredible shot-making skills to force a third and deciding set. As Brandon and I reviewed our match strategy during the set break, I told him how proud I was of him, and that he should be very proud of himself as well. "Now, isn't this fun?" I asked. He agreed and was excited to play the final set of his high school career. In the third set, both players exhibited brilliant play and extreme toughness, and spectators told me they hardly recognized Brandon—his attitude and behavior were exceptional, a truly remarkable turnaround from the way they remembered him. Both players exhibited respect for the game and each other, which was evident in the match. They both wanted badly to win, but Brandon was beaten, 7–5. As he walked toward the net to shake hands, I had that scary vision of Brandon throwing his racket at his bag as a freshman. I watched him closely as he shook hands, hugged, and congratulated his opponent. I breathed a huge sigh of relief. Then Brandon walked to his tennis bag, sat down, and began to cry. His teammates entered the court, congratulated the winner, then sat next to Brandon, watching their captain and not knowing what to say to him. I congratulated his opponent myself, walked over to Brandon and put my hand on his shoulder, crying myself.

"Coach," Brandon said, "I'm so sorry I let you down."

"Brandon, you didn't let me down in any way." I told him. "In fact, I'm more proud of you right now than ever, because you represented me, the team, and our school with such class.

We win a lot, but to get beat in that situation, under that kind of adversity, and to demonstrate the character you did—that speaks louder than any victory. This is what our team is all about."

Then I took a walk around the tennis complex, reflecting on Brandon's high school career. I felt so fulfilled that we were able to help him go from the bad end of the spectrum during his freshman year to the good end as he neared graduation. It was also clear to me that if Brandon had had better discipline when he was younger, rather than working on it for the first time in high school, he would have been playing at a much higher level now. But better late than never.

I received so many compliments from spectators who watched that championship final about the way Brandon represented himself and our team. What's more, he set a great example in leadership for our younger players, who saw firsthand the importance of attitude and behavior, especially in defeat. Seeing Brandon's character in action is something his teammates could strive for. And that would influence not only how they performed on the court but, more important, how they represented themselves, their team, their school, and their families. This was real winning. This was real success.

CHAPTER 12

SUSTAINING SUCCESS

"Even if you're on the right track,
you'll get run over if you just sit there."
—Will Rogers

I t's definitely much easier to climb to the top of a mountain than it is to stay there. Some athletes want to achieve mastery in their sport, but every team wants to win a championship and be number one. Everyone in business wants to be number one. That's completely fine and natural. I was able to lead my teams in winning 22 consecutive state championships by using the Four Ps—people, purpose, process, equals performance. If you build good relationships with people, have a clear purpose in wanting to achieve something meaningful together, and follow a detailed process to accomplish it, you will directly influence your team's performance.

These Four Ps are critical in getting consistent results, and the Eight Keys to achieving success provide ways to put your team in the best position to be successful and sustain that success. In Chapter 4, we saw that character improvement is essential in establishing a foundation on which team members can build and must be every leader's number one priority. As leader, you will teach them the skills necessary for continued development in their sport or business to improve their skills. Having good character traits is the foundation in striving to win a championship and to have the chance to sustain a championship streak.

The same is true in business. Say you're launching a new company—you hire the right staff in part by making sure they're all of good character. Their character will be a reflection on you. Then you identify the purpose and mission of the team and articulate why it's important to strive for these goals together. Then comes the individual training, including introducing the tools necessary to conduct your business on a day-to-day basis. When you can help your team members improve both internally and externally in this way, it directly affects their performance in getting the results you want. The Four Ps provide the framework and the Eight Keys provide the details in achieving and sustaining success.

Outdo Your Accomplishments

Several years ago I was a guest speaker at a sports forum in Honolulu. An audience member asked about our national record of winning the most consecutive state championships in U.S. history in any sport, and how I accomplished it. I shared two specific details with the audience.

First, we need to outdo what we've already done. Winning a state championship this year doesn't guarantee that we'll win one next year—let alone 22 years in a row. Yesterday's home runs don't win tomorrow's games. We need to be stronger, faster, smarter, and better than we were the previous year. We cannot be complacent. We need to improve our conditioning, footwork, and flexibility. We need to get physically stronger in the weight room and do what it takes to prevent injuries. We need to control our internal climate no matter how noisy and crazy the match. We need to add more strategies and tactics. We need to execute better, becoming more consistent with our shots and adding power at the right times. We need to improve our nutrition. We must have a constant striving for excellence and better ourselves as tennis players and people every day. It's human nature to believe that, once you achieve victory or success, it's time to relax a little. We cannot relax.

Because we have a successful framework and process in place, others can see that it works and try to emulate us.

Second, we can never take any opponent for granted. We need to be prepared to play anyone. We are the target. We're the ones with the X on our backs. Other teams are excited to play us because they have nothing to lose. This is scary because such an opposing team could play at an extraordinary level. They can be loose and relaxed, with no real expectations of winning—until they're near the end of a match and find themselves in a great position to win. They might be playing in the zone, feeling no pressure and with everything to gain. Throw in huge crowd support for the other team and our own players not playing up to their capability, and we could very well lose. But isn't this what makes sports exciting? You don't play the game on paper. You play it in person, face to face. There might be a favorite and an underdog or two evenly matched teams playing each other, but the team that usually wins is the one with a solid foundation in discipline and character.

Building a championship team is challenging enough. But how do you then sustain that position by winning again the following year, and the year after that, and the one after that? I always look at the end result I want, and then work backwards to help the team understand what's necessary to achieve that result. It's important to break things down in detail.

For example, in order to win a tennis match, a player needs to win two sets. Before he can win two sets, he needs to win one set. In order to win that set, he needs to win six games. Before he wins six games, he needs to win one game. To win that game, he needs to win four points. Before winning those four points, he needs to win one point. And the only way you have a chance in winning that first point is in practice, right here, right now. That's how important practices really are.

Your team members need to understand this, and it's easier to them to see when you break it down and work your way backward toward reaching the goal. It's important for your coaching staff and players to understand that whether you won or lost the last point, the most important thing now is the next one. Understanding this is crucial, so that the athlete can maintain his present focus and be at his best for the next point. After all, that's the one thing he can control that will affect whether he wins or loses. And being at his best for the next point depends on what he does in practice, right here, right now. Making a shot in basketball can earn you two points, or three if you're behind the arc. But in tennis, as in baseball, volleyball, and soccer, it's one point, one run, one goal at a time; there are no three-pointers.

Everything should focus on that next point. Training your athletes to give their best physically, mentally, and emotionally for each and every point or play makes all the difference. This is the mentality that must be instilled in practice, so that your athletes can perform when it really counts in competition. It all depends on disciplined practice and proper training. The athlete needs to understand that they must practice the same way they play. Practice does not make perfect. What if you're practicing the wrong things? Perfect practices give them the chance to achieve their goals. Great effort, fun, a positive attitude, and enjoying and helping each other in practice are necessary in building this habit for competition. My own practices are designed to be tough so that playing matches feels much easier. And another thing: If players are getting too fatigued in matches, then they probably aren't preparing correctly enough in practice.

Strengths vs. Weaknesses

Having a complete game gives you more opportunities to execute more strategies. How can you beat a better athlete or a team that's favored over yours? That's where the concept of the upset comes in. That's why athletic competitions aren't played on paper but on the field or court. So how do you manage it? You use your strengths and attack their weaknesses. If your opponent doesn't have any visible weakness, they will still prefer to compete against a certain kind of opponent.

Most everyone has a type of opponent that they'd rather play, and also a type that they'd rather *not* compete against.

In tennis, for example, there are four shot preferences. Does my opponent like high or low balls? Does he like deep or short balls? Does he like hard or soft shots? Does he like shots out wide or into the body? By figuring out your opponent's preferences, you can establish an effective strategy and put yourself in the most favorable position to win. You don't have to be better than your opponent at everything. You just need to be better at *one* thing and do that thing over and over again. You're not going to win every point or every game, but your focus should be on trying to win the majority of them. You aren't in it for a sprint; you're in it for a marathon.

Most tennis matches are lost rather than won. It's not the big plays you make. It's the errors you don't make. It's more important for players and teams to work toward having zero weaknesses. You might not have many strengths, but having no weaknesses always puts you in a favorable position to win. And then, ideally, you will develop new strengths along the way.

Weaknesses can be physical, mental, emotional, tactical, environmental, or strategic. I often use the analogy of a person sitting in a boat with several holes in the bottom. These holes represent a player's weaknesses, which need to be addressed and worked on immediately and concurrently. In competition, that player might be performing well and thereby plugging one or two of the holes, but he might still be sinking because of other deficiencies against a quality opponent. Can you imagine how much better this athlete would perform if all the holes are plugged? He'll keep his head above water and his boat afloat. It's your job as coach to identify your player's weaknesses and help plug the holes in their development.

One Play at a Time

On January 2, 2016, the University of Oregon football team played Texas Christian University in the Alamo Bowl. In the week before the game, TCU's coach had suspended his starting quarterback for off-field issues. By halftime, Oregon was dominating, 31–0. But then Oregon's quarterback was injured and didn't play the rest of the game. Now both teams were competing with their backup quarterbacks. In the second half, TCU—seemingly unfazed by the huge deficit—played the game one snap at a time, coming all the way back to tie the Ducks at 31–31. They then prevailed in triple overtime and won by a score of 47–41. It was an amazing comeback for TCU and a devastating loss for Oregon.

In sports you're always in one of three situations—winning, losing, or tied. The effort and positive attitude to give it your best should always be there, regardless of the score. Too many teams play according to the score, which can easily bring their downfall. It can be a self-fulfilling prophecy. Obviously you want to be aware of the score, but you don't want it to change your strategy if you're winning. If you're behind, you clearly need to alter or change your strategy. And if you're tied, your strategy might well be sound—you're in a position to win, but it will depend on your execution. Here's where having discipline and training in practice puts you and your team in a more favorable position to come out ahead.

Sustaining success requires a mindset of performing one play at a time, or one point at a time, regardless of the score or any other circumstances. In tennis, I've seen many players win the first set but end up losing the match because they relax and lose focus. They think that because they've won that first set, they're well on their way to victory. A football team with a substantial lead at the end of the third quarter might relax and lose focus. A volleyball team leading the match two sets to none might relax and lose focus. As a tennis player, I've experienced both sides—jumping out ahead but losing the match, and falling behind but emerging victorious. Anyone who plays sports has had the same experience.

I constantly remind my players that it doesn't really matter who wins the first set. If we do, it only means we're ahead but haven't won. If we drop the first set, we're behind but still haven't lost. I want them to have the mindset of playing one point at a time. I want them to give it their best from the first point until match point. I want them to play the whole match. I want them to run the whole marathon. When you train your team to have this mindset, they become relentless competitors who control everything that they're able to control. And your opponent might have some mental lapses along the way, which of course puts you in a more favorable position to win.

Dominate the In-Between

Sustaining success also involves controlling your thoughts between plays or between points. A football game can last three hours or more, even though actual playing time is just 60 minutes. In tennis a match of two out of three sets might last for two or three hours, but the actual amount of time the ball is in play might be only 15 or 20 minutes. The point is there's lots of time between plays or between points when our minds might wander and lose focus, which impacts how we play the next point. Controlling our thoughts between points is important. Our teams work on a routine to use between when the previous point ends and the next one begins. This is extremely critical in giving your best from the first point until match point. At high levels of play, just one mental lapse can make you lose the match. Controlling our thoughts, giving our best effort, having the right attitude, and keeping proper focus are disciplines we have total control over between points. This discipline, this habit, adds to our relentless competitive play in matches, which helps us attain success and sustain it too.

I always emphasize to my teams that we must exhibit positivity, toughness, and fight regardless of whether we won or lost the last point. Obviously, you wouldn't have a negative response if you won the point, but it's very easy for average players to show negativity, frustration, and disappointment after losing one. It takes a lot of self-discipline to shake it off, and to keep in mind that a negative response won't help you win the next point. In fact, it will help you lose it. This is all common sense, of course, but in the heat of the battle, anything can and will happen to undisciplined players. The disciplined ones will keep it together because their leader has trained them to do so. Disciplined players will focus on the present. They won't stress about what just happened (past focus) and they won't worry about what could happen (future focus). This is something the leader has trained his or her team members to control.

Players have a choice to show either strength or weakness between points. Players have a choice to show positivity or negativity. Players have a choice to show toughness or frustration. Players have a choice to show fight or to give up. It's easy to lose a point and show weakness, negativity, and frustration, to make excuses and ultimately give up. It's very challenging to lose a point, have complete self-control and show strength, positivity, toughness, and fight. But this is what great teams do. This is what great organizations do. In order to sustain success, the leader will analyze every little detail of every situation and guide the team into the best possible position to sustain success.

The Robbie Lim Story

My players always look forward to my "world famous quote of the day." I know my quotes inspired Robbie Lim to become a great player, leader, and teammate. In fact, Robbie began using his own inspirational quotes from movies to inspire and motivate his teammates. I loved it, not only because it was entertaining watching him imitate Al Pacino in *Any Given Sunday*, for instance, but also because it was meaningful to his teammates.

Robbie Lim went from being a follower to a leader right before my eyes. Sharing those quotes, having discipline and following our process, along with a good foundation of character traits he already had to build on, led Robbie to be one of the best team captains we ever had. One thing you need to know about him: He had average talent in tennis and was an average athlete as well. His younger brother and sister, who both played in Punahou's tennis program, had much more natural talent than he did. But what made Robbie special was his character, mental toughness, and smart play. As a sophomore in 2002, Robbie won the state singles championship in Wailea, Maui. He was seeded fourth in the tournament but still went on to be a young singles champion, for all those reasons.

The following year, when he was a junior and our team captain, Robbie created some memorable stories that I could share with my teams for years to come. He went undefeated during our regular season, won the league championship in singles, and was the number one seed at the state championship tournament held on O'ahu. In the quarterfinals, he faced 'Iolani School's number one player on the stadium court. It was an unusually hot, humid and windless day, and what's more, the stadium court is sunken, which makes it the hottest court in the entire facility. Both players had won earlier matches that day in the round of sixteen. Robbie's opponent was a tall, talented player who was a very tough competitor. Each athlete wanted to beat the other very badly and was willing to endure these extreme conditions. The match started with both players hitting extremely hard, heavy shots. Both of them were exhibiting exceptional footwork. But then things began to change for the worse. Robbie had won the first set and his opponent the second. At the start of the third set, they both began suffering painfully debilitating cramps almost simultaneously. What had looked like a high-level championship contest soon took on the appearance of a ten-and-under match. Robbie and his opponent moaned and groaned with every step they took to get to the ball. When they did hit the ball, it was a soft lob shot traveling no faster than two miles an hour. They were both giving it all they had, and neither player would give up and retire the match. They continued playing in this way and the match passed the three-hour mark. For those of us on the sidelines, it was almost as painful to watch. Finally, Robbie won the set, limped up to the net to shake hands, and then immediately sought out the trainers. Both players were lying side by side on the trainers' tables, receiving fluids and ice treatments. Soon after, Robbie's parents took him to the hospital for an IV.

That evening Robbie called. When I asked how he was feeling, he said, "Not so good, Coach. I think I might have to default my semifinal tomorrow." For a skinny kid, Robbie was also very tough, so the possibility of a default showed me just how much pain he was feeling. He didn't think his body could recover in time, even after the IV. But I told him to get a good night's sleep and see how he felt in the morning—and to mentally plan to be ready to play his 8 a.m. semifinal.

When Robbie arrived the next day, things didn't look good. He appeared weak and wasn't his normal, upbeat self. Even walking looked difficult, and I could only imagine how he'd feel playing tennis in this condition. He asked what I thought he should do. I told him that since he was here, he might as well try to play. "If it gets too bad," I said, "you can retire the match." He agreed and took the court without even warming up.

Robbie's opponent was strong and talented—the number one player for Kahuku High School. From the start, the match wasn't pretty to watch. Robbie could barely move six feet in any direction and had problems hitting more than two or three shots per point. His opponent was serving and returning serves very well and was clearly dictating play. It was as if Robbie had his hands tied behind his back and was taking punches one after another. His opponent won the first set 6–1, and I went on court to talk with Robbie during the 90-second coaching break. We actually shared a laugh that he was able to win one game. I asked him if he wanted to retire the match, but he said he wanted to stay out there and show his opponent some respect, even though he was being outplayed and felt extremely weak.

As I started to leave the court, I asked Robbie, "Who's the champ?"

"I'm the champ," he said in a soft whisper.

"Who's the champ?"

"I'm the champ," he said again, sounding a little more convinced this time.

"Yes, you are the champ," I answered, "and champs give everything they've got, with no excuses. You need to stay out here as long as you can. You never know—you might begin to feel better. Now, who's the champ?"

"I'm the champ!"

"All right, champ," I said as I walked off the court. "Go!"

I hoped that Robbie might somehow find a way to turn things around, but as they started the second set, he still looked bad. I mean, *really* bad. Hope faded quickly as the Kahuku player executed shot after shot and point after point, while Robbie, though still standing, almost seemed to be losing his pulse. Down 2–5 in the second set, Robbie got up from a water break to switch ends of the court. He was now one game away from losing, after winning the state championship the previous year.

Standing by the fence, I yelled, "Who's the champ?"

Robbie walked closer and said, "I'm the champ!"—all of a sudden with a look on his face I hadn't seen the whole match.

"Who's the champ?" I asked again.

"Coach," he said, "I'm the champ!"

And then—wow! Did he start to come alive! He began bouncing on his feet, moving faster to each shot, and producing more pace on every one. After being close to losing his pulse, Robbie was finally showing some real life. But was it too little too late? After holding off three match points, Robbie tied the second set at 5–5, and his opponent began making unforced errors. Now Robbie was looking like his normal self again, and he won the second set, 7–5.

You can only imagine what the spectators were thinking. I walked back on court during the ten-minute coaching break that follows split sets. I congratulated him on his comeback, and on his will in finding a way to win. He hadn't won yet, but I could see the determined fight in him. He'd been on the ropes with both hands tied behind his back, almost ready for a knockout, but now here he was at even sets and just a couple of minutes away from starting the third.

"Who's the champ?" I asked as we stood facing each other, bouncing on our feet in unison.

"I'm the champ!" he answered with tenacity. We shook hands and hugged, and I walked off the court.

The third and deciding set was sure to be a battle. The spectators became more vocal, applauding the brilliant shot making and the effort and will to win by both players. Loud cheers erupted for both players after every point.

Robbie won the third set, 6–0. It was remarkable. It was inspiring to his teammates and everyone who witnessed it. You hear people say never give up. But actually seeing those words in action makes them so much more meaningful. In tennis, time cannot run out. You need to win a certain number of points to win. There is no stalling. There are no time-outs. There are no substitutions. (Although believe me, I wish we were allowed substitutions; I could have used them many times over the years.) Robbie's performance was truly remarkable. Most players in his situation would have retired the match after losing that first set. But not Robbie—understanding his place as the defending champion, wanting to honor and respect his opponent by staying on the court even if he was going to lose, speaks volumes about his character. And remember, this was only the semifinal. He had only a one-hour rest break before he played in the state championship final.

During that break, Robbie experienced both intense focus and great excitement about playing in the final match. But his opponent, a Farrington High School player who was seeded number two, was also looking extremely confident. He was a strong, talented lefty who hit heavy topspin shots and moved extremely well. It was definitely shaping up to be an epic contest, especially because the Farrington kid had dominated his semifinal match and had had much more time to relax and recover while Robbie made his dramatic comeback.

This worried me. How would Robbie perform after

expending so much physical, mental, and emotional energy? Would he have enough drive and determination to defend and earn a second state singles championship? Would our months of preparation and discipline be the little variable that made a big difference in the final outcome?

As he and his opponent began their five-minute warm-up with each other, spectators crowded into every open space, filling in row after row around the court. Once the match started, both players were looking really good. It actually seemed that each was playing his best tennis of the tournament. That's always a great thing to see, and it doesn't happen as often as we'd like. Robbie and the Farrington player had very similar styles of play: They were aggressive baseliners with consistent serves and return of serves, and they were each trying to attack the other's backhand.

But from the start, Robbie dominated—and won the match, 6–0, 6–0. Midway through the contest, a sports writer for *The Honolulu Advertiser* found me and told me she couldn't believe what she was witnessing. She said it was incredible watching Robbie compete and win his second state singles championship. I told her that what was most incredible was that he'd been one game away from losing in the semifinals—and then went on to win 23 straight games to take the championship. Robbie earned the respect of everyone there that day. He respected his opponents and competed with class, whether he was winning, losing, or tied. It had been an amazing display of character and heart. As his coach, I would have felt proud of Robbie regardless of the outcome. But he reinforced himself as a leader among his peers and gave me yet another memorable story to share with our future teams and players.

Heart is something that can be very difficult to see and measure. It often manifests itself only in times of extreme stress and adversity. You never know how strong a person really is until his back is against a wall. And it's a beautiful thing to see when it shows itself in players during competition. All great leaders have heart. It was evident that Robbie had heart.

Teammates admire a leader's standard of excellence and are happy to follow someone who knows where he or she is going.

A coach can lead effectively with a big heart and a high standard of excellence, demanding the same from every member of the team. Of course, a team captain like Robbie Lim can help facilitate the coach's expectations, discipline, and goals, but it starts with the coach. Talking the talk is fine, but you really earn respect from your team by walking the walk every single day. 🎾

CHAPTER 13

WHAT IS YOUR LEGACY?

*"One day you'll be just a memory for some people.
Do your best to be a good one."*
—Anonymous

I miss coaching my boys' varsity tennis team. It was a huge part of my life for 22 years. When a season ended, I always looked forward to the next one, excited to see which 12 boys would earn their spots on the team.

Still, it was only 12 boys that I could help. It was only 12 boys that would be a part of a great team experience that year. I retired as head coach in 2015 because I felt compelled to do something bigger. I felt that, rather than coaching at just one school, helping just 12 boys each season, maybe there was a way I could help many more of them.

And then a friend and former student urged me to find a way to help people not just in sports, but also in business. Having gone through my program, he believed that I was much more than a tennis coach. I was a leader, he said, who had developed a process that could unlock people's true potential, the same process that forged our unprecedented 22-year championship streak. It's the same process he uses in his own company, with his own team. He knows it works because he has lived it himself, as have many of my students and players. That's when and why I decided to write this book.

Achievement vs. Fulfillment

Of course, a legacy doesn't happen when you're the only one who's affected. It happens when you help others, affecting them in a positive way. It happens when you help people grow and improve themselves. It happens when you guide them in following their dreams. That's why being on a team means more than accomplishing something on your own. You share the highs and lows together. You share the struggles and victories together. You help each other be better people together.

Fulfillment happens when you do things for others without expecting anything in return. In our society, status, beauty, money, power, fame, and material things like big, beautiful houses and fancy cars are high on the wish list for most people. But do they ultimately bring happiness at the same time? Many of these people find that they're lonely and unhappy, that there's something missing on the inside. They have everything that you can possibly imagine externally, but they lack self-fulfillment internally.

So if we identify character traits in detail and prioritize the ones that are most important in achieving self-fulfillment, I believe it is our moral traits that should top the list. Focusing on mental and emotional character traits is important, of course, but focusing on moral traits will help your team members feel most fulfilled.

- Examples of moral character include integrity, honor, loyalty, humility, respect for others, caring, and compassion.

- Examples of mental character include discipline, focus, decisiveness, ambition, dedication, self-control, adaptability, and self-awareness.

- Examples of emotional character include positivity, resiliency, confidence, understanding, cooperation, and courage.

Certainly all of these traits are important, but which of them should we ultimately strive for? Which of these should we instill in our team members? I strongly believe that having moral character brings the most fulfillment and happiness. I have seen it. As a coach, I am most proud of players who acquire many, if not all, of these character traits, whether or not they win or lose a competition. This is what I wanted to establish on my first day as head coach—helping my team realize that we develop great people first and great tennis players second. I had no idea when I began my coaching career that this is what I would accomplish. This would be my legacy. This is why, till this day, I refer to my old Creighton mentor as Coach Ed and likewise, my players still call me Coach. It denotes the respect that team members have for their leader.

Own No Trophies

Hawai'i's state championship trophy is big and absolutely beautiful. I've been presented that trophy 22 times, but today not one of them is in my possession. Each year I gave the state championship trophy to the one player I felt significantly represented our team with the highest standards of excellence. What good would it do for me to hold on to 22 trophies? It means more to me for the players to have them. I felt happy and fulfilled in giving the trophy to those 22 athletes, as a symbol of the meaning of their teams' accomplishments. It's a constant reminder of the way that commitment, sacrifice, teamwork, perseverance, resiliency, and discipline can help you achieve your goal. It's something special that they were a part of, and no one can take that away.

Sure, trophies are great to have. It's a symbol of victory. It's a symbol of being a winner. But it's also a symbol of something much deeper and greater. What did you have to do to get that victory? Why did you win? The trophy represents the countless hours and hard work involved in pursuing that goal. It is a symbol of sweat and pain. It is a symbol of sacrifice and commitment and never giving up even when your back is against the wall. It is a symbol of all the other people involved in giving you an opportunity to succeed—parents who drove you to practices and games, teammates who worked together and encouraged each other to give their best every day. It is so much more than just something you can look at and hold—it is something that's embedded deep in your soul.

The Jimmy V. Story

In 1983 Jim Valvano, head coach of the North Carolina State men's basketball team, led his team to the NCAA national championship. It would be his only championship win, yet his legacy with his team members extended way beyond the basketball court. Some years later, Jimmy V. was diagnosed with cancer and gave one of the most memorable speeches I've ever heard, on the night he received the Arthur Ashe Award at the 1993 ESPY Awards. "Cancer can affect much of my physical body," he said that evening, "but it cannot touch my mind, it cannot touch my heart, and it cannot touch my soul." He also said, "Time is precious and you don't know how much time you have left." Jimmy V. passed away eight weeks later.

If you haven't seen his speech, I highly recommend that you find it on YouTube and watch it. Obviously he was a great basketball coach, but he clearly had a passion for life that helped his players on the court and ultimately helped them in their lives as well. His legacy was far-reaching, including the establishment of his V Foundation for Cancer Research. This one person, this one leader, impacted and helped improve the lives of so many people beyond basketball.

The Mikey MacKinnon Story

You never know when you will be a part of someone else's legacy. I started private tennis lessons with a seventh grade student named Mikey MacKinnon. After our first two lessons, I was able to observe him in a junior team tennis match. This was the longest tennis match I've ever seen. The format was just an eight-game pro-set but it lasted for three hours. Yes, three hours! Mikey moved very well and had very good shot consistency. His consistency was so good that it looked like he enjoyed extending tennis points by torturing his opponent with shots hit at no more than five miles per hour.

Mikey's opponent wasn't the only one being tortured; I endured having to watch identical points being played over and over again. Mikey won the match 8–2. At our next lesson, I told Mikey that we were going to work on turning him into an aggressive baseliner. It was imperative for him to learn power. Plus, he could thank me for saving him hours of time to do other things—like homework!

In 1998, Mikey was a senior on my varsity team. He was number one on the team and ranked number two in the state of Hawaiʻi. He was a great team player and was well-liked by everyone. He listened well, worked extremely hard, and had lots of fun.

One day during a varsity match against a smaller school, I played a weaker lineup and had Mikey practicing with three of his teammates on court two. During the match, I heard Mikey yelling, "Coach, come quick!" and saw him holding his right bicep. Fearing an injury, I ran over to court two to find out what happened. Mikey walked up to me, moaning slightly and still holding his arm. Then he rolled up his shirt sleeves and flexed his muscles. "Coach, my muscles—they're too big! They're breaking out of my skin!" I shook my head and laughed, relieved that he wasn't really injured.

Later that season, Mikey was playing in the state singles championship final against the number one ranked player in the state, a boy from Maui. Everyone was expecting an epic showdown from these top two seeds in the tournament. Throughout the first set, the level of tennis was extremely high, with both players hitting exceptional shots and giving every ounce of energy they had. But in what seemed to take only about 15 minutes, Mikey lost the first set, 6–0. I walked onto the court to talk with him during the 90-second coaching break. I told Mikey that he was playing and competing very well, and that his opponent couldn't keep playing in the zone like that for two whole sets. He had for one set, and maybe could for a set and a half, but unlikely for two.

I walked off the court, excited to see what would happen. Both players continued to make brilliant shots, but I'd been wrong. Mikey's opponent was still playing in the zone and beat him 6–0 in the second set. Then, after walking to the net to shake the winner's hand, Mikey stayed near the court, sitting in the shade. Everyone who'd watched the match was in complete shock—myself included. I could only imagine what Mikey would be feeling after playing the last match of his high school career and having it end as it did. I sat down next to him and the first thing he said was, "How is first doubles and the other guys doing?"

"They're doing good," I replied. "How are you, Mikey?"

"I'm OK," he said. "Wow, did my opponent play awesome or what?"

"Yes, he was awesome," I agreed. "He probably could have beaten anyone in the state today."

And that was it. Mikey picked up his bag and went over to cheer on his teammates who were still competing. To do that after suffering this lopsided defeat shows you the kind of person he was. He was a leader and a role model, and he knew that the team was bigger than any one person.

After the season ended, I continued to train Mikey in private and group lessons to prepare him for college tennis. He was excited to work on improving his tennis, as well as having fun with his friends at the beach. But one Sunday that summer, he didn't show up for our group training lesson. Now, you need to understand that Mikey was always there for his lessons, even when he was sick, so we all knew that there was something unusual going on. When I finished our training and drove home, I called his house. His dad answered the phone.

"Scott," I said, "Mikey never came to training today."

"Rusty, Mikey died today—a car accident."

No words came—I was in shock. "Coach," I finally heard Scott ask, "are you OK?" His dad was trying to comfort *me*. I could only try to imagine what he and his family were going through.

Mikey's parents are incredible people, as is his older brother, Rob, and younger sister, Heather. They asked me if I'd speak at Mikey's memorial at the Punahou School chapel, and I felt honored to do so. At the service, every seat was taken, with an overflow of people spilling outside. I had prepared four pages of memories about Mikey to share. But when I walked to the podium, adjusted the microphone, and tried to speak, I couldn't get out more than a word or two. My emotions overwhelmed me, and I broke down in tears. Everyone in the chapel began crying along with me. Rob came up to the podium, put his hand on my shoulder and said, "Coach, you can do this." And I did. It was the hardest thing I ever had to do.

The MacKinnon family started a scholarship fund at the school in Mikey's memory. The scholarship is awarded to three students each year. One is a player on the boys' varsity tennis team. Another is a tennis player, boy or girl, in the Punahou academy (high school level). And a third is presented to a tennis player, boy or girl, in the middle school. In this way, Mikey's legacy is carried forward. Each year, the MacKinnon family and some of Mikey's teammates and I gather at a luncheon with the three new Mike MacKinnon scholarship winners, where we're able to share with them the kind of person Mikey was. It is a most special legacy, and I'm honored to be part of it. 🎾

---◆---

FINDING GREATNESS

I n these pages, we've learned eight keys for achieving and sustaining success in a team environment—in sports, in business or in any other arena. When you instill these principles in your team, you're well on your way to creating a legacy for others to follow. When you think big, you can accomplish big things in life. You aren't inventing anything new, you're just taking what you may already be doing to a much higher level. I firmly believe that focusing on the Four Ps and the Eight Keys put my teams in the best position to be successful, to win those 22 consecutive championships and most important, to be great people.

The many parallels in leadership between sports and business are clear. There's really no difference between a coaching job and a management position—in both roles you're leading people. A parent, of course, is the original leader. What a better world this would be if every parent instilled in every child character development, discipline, strategies for control, courage, creating a positive environment, pursuing passions, handling adversity, and increasing the odds for a successful life? These eight keys need to be practiced and reinforced consistently to enhance the performance—and the lives—of your team members. This should be the legacy that *you* leave— encouraging them to move on and share their own priceless experiences and stories with those who they will influence in turn.

Inspiring and helping your team shows them, by example, how to inspire and help others. I challenge you to instill in your team members the belief that they can be greater than they think.

I know there is greatness in you. It is there in all of us. Find yours, then help others find theirs.

ABOUT THE AUTHOR

Rusty Komori is a motivational speaker, leadership consultant, and tennis professional based in Honolulu, Hawai'i. From 1994 through 2015, he was the head tennis coach at Punahou School, where his boys' varsity teams won an unprecedented 22 consecutive state championships, a national record in all sports that still stands. Rusty can be reached via his website, www.rustykomori.com.